WHEN WALLS COME TUMBLING DOWN

WHEN WALLS COME TUMBLING DOWN

Experiencing God's Power to Break Through Barriers

Deborah P. Brunt

New Hope
Birmingham, Alabama

New Hope
P. O. Box 12065
Birmingham, Alabama 35202-2065

Cover design by Barry Graham

Dewey Decimal Classification: 248.4
Subject Headings: CHRISTIAN LIFE
                  PRAYER
                  MISSIONS—PERSONAL
                  NARRATIVE

ISBN: 1-56309-093-7
N944111•0494•5M1

CONTENTS

INTRODUCTION

"Behold, I have put before you an open door which no one can shut" (Rev. 3:8a NASB).

Monday morning, 6:00 A.M., as usual the clock-radio roused me. But instead of hearing music, I caught the end of a news bulletin. "The Jews will probably leave in large numbers, now that Gorbachev is no longer in power," the announcer said.

My stomach did a flip. *Leave where?* I thought. *What's going on? And what does it mean for our trip?*

I knew the mood in the Soviet Union was volatile. President Mikhail Gorbachev was trying to give the 15 republics some freedoms while still holding the reins. Several republics were demanding more independence than he was offering. I feared one or more of them had revolted.

All this news was personal for me. I was supposed to leave two weeks from that day for a trip to the Soviet cities of Moscow, Yalta, and Bishkek, with a team of young women called Enterprisers. We planned to distribute 70,000 Russian New Testaments.

As music began to play on the radio, I jumped out of bed, ran to the den, turned on the TV, and flipped the channel to CNN. My heart sank. On the screen, I saw Moscow's streets—with tanks rolling down them. It was August 19, 1991. I was watching the Soviet coup.

The evening before, Gorbachev had been "detained" while vacationing in Yalta. Hard-line Communist party leaders, announcing that Gorbachev was ill, placed the nation in a "state of emergency" and declared themselves in charge.

Learning of the coup at dawn on Monday, Russian president Boris

1

Yeltsin made his way to the Russian parliament building in downtown Moscow. In remarkable displays of courage, he declared to the press, the people, the coup leaders, and the military that the coup was "madness." He urged the people to stand with him against it.

Citizens began to respond. For the next two days, they poured into Moscow's streets. Surrounding the White House, they built barricades to try to protect Yeltsin. Meeting incoming tanks and military units, they urged soldiers not to fight against their own people.

That Monday morning, the situation looked worse than bleak. I watched, unbelieving, as coverage continued and "experts" debated the outcome. "Coups can fail," said some, including President George Bush.[1] "Remember Tiananmen Square," others argued. "If the military decides to get tough, the people are doomed."

When I knew more than enough and could summon the energy to stand up and turn off the TV, I plodded back through the bedroom on my way to the bathroom.

"Anything wrong?" my half-asleep husband, Jerry, called from the bed.

"Twenty-four hundred dollars down the drain," I answered.

Dashed Hopes

Actually, much more than money was at stake. For one thing, about half my expenses for the trip had been furnished by donations from fellow church members. If I could not make the trip, I felt I would be letting down those who invested in me. I had spent more than 50 hours training for the trip and had secured several items necessary for making the journey, but not needed otherwise.

As a result of a weekly newspaper column I write, 30 people in my community had made written commitments to pray for every aspect of the trip. Seven people (in addition to Jerry) had signed up for baby-sitting stints during the 11 days I would be gone for orientation and the trip itself. Others had volunteered to be backup sitters or to bring meals to my family. Children in my church had gathered small goodies for our group to take as gifts to the Soviet people.

My going was a group effort. If I didn't go, it would mean a group disappointment. Multiply that disappointment by the 24 other members of the Enterprisers team, as well as 34 more adults of both sexes and all ages who would travel and minister alongside us—then multiply that number times their families and friends and prayer partners.

That's a lot of dashed hopes. Yet I realized that our letdown was nothing compared to the dashed hopes the Soviet peoples would experience if the freedoms they had tasted so briefly were now brutally withdrawn. As I thought and rethought the matter that whole day and the next, I decided the real question was not, Will I go? but, Will all those Bibles get into the hands of people whose eternal destiny hinges on their learning the truth?

Our mission to take 70,000 Bibles into three Soviet cities was part of a large interdenominational effort sponsored in part by the International Bible Society and the Evangelical Christian Publishers Association. The goal was to provide 4 million Russian New Testaments to a people deprived of the truth for more than 70 years. Other Christian organizations were also trying to work quickly to channel the gospel to the Soviet Union's 290 million people while the doors were still open. If hard-line communism now ruled again, all those efforts would abruptly end.

For two days, I was numb. All the last-minute preparations I'd been rushing to make came to a halt. I completed other duties as required, but spent as much time as I could in front of the TV, watching the story unfold.

Many people who knew about my upcoming trip asked, "You won't be able to go now, will you?"

"It doesn't look like it," I answered. I had heard nothing from our trip leaders. I didn't try to call them. I felt I would know something when *they* knew something.

Splintered Door

Later, I learned that some team members were ready to go on, regardless of what was happening; but the US State Department was advising Americans to stay away from the Soviet turmoil. Unless conditions changed dramatically, our sending agency would surely cancel the trip.

Amazingly, I didn't feel frustrated, discouraged, or angry; but I was confused. I took my confusion to the Lord. "Father," I said, "when I was praying about whether to make this trip, I read Revelation 3:8, 'Behold, I have put before you an open door which no one can shut' (NASB). You used that verse to call me.

"Yet now the door appears closed, and there doesn't seem to be any way it can open again in time for us to leave for Moscow in two weeks. The plans have to be made or canceled now. You know that, Father.

"So I just lift up to You the verse You gave me. I don't know what it means in this situation, but I'm continuing to claim it."

In my newspaper column that week, I wrote, "I don't plan to beat down any doors. Or even to push hard against those I find closed. But what God opens, I will walk through."

Tuesday, the tension built to a climax. That night before going to bed, I watched the news. The first shots had been fired; three young men were killed.

Wednesday morning, I awoke to find that the coup seemed to be unraveling. Coup leaders were trying to flee the country. On orders from the Defense Ministry, all troops were clearing out of Moscow. Rumor had it that Gorbachev was back in power and would soon be returning to Moscow.

All morning, I listened to news of the rapidly failing coup. All morning, I cried. Later reports credited Yeltsin, the Russian people, and the incompetency of the coup leaders with the coup's failure. I knew those were important factors. But I also knew where the real credit lay: Almighty God had opened a door that no one could shut.

By noon, I received word, "The trip is on." Many of my friends and family members were skeptical about our going, with conditions in the Soviet Union still so unsettled; but nothing short of total incapacity could have stopped me from making that trip.

I had seen the Lord of breakthrough splinter a door of iron. The force of His blow had shattered the government of the world's largest nation, had changed the lives of more than 290 million people overnight, and had sent shock waves ricocheting around the world. What a privilege to have a tiny part in His great work!

Echoing Cry

This book is about that breakthrough—and more. It's an in-depth look at a phenomenon people long to see, whether in a way that shakes the world or a way that changes one life.

In these ten chapters, you'll learn:
- what hinders breakthrough—and what unleashes it;
- how to wait for breakthrough—and what to do if it never comes;
- how to recognize breakthrough—and how to handle it.

Throughout the book, you'll find biblical principles. You'll meet real people who've seen those principles work.

Maybe you don't need a breakthrough. Maybe no one you know does. But I doubt it.

One man I interviewed while gathering material for this book sent me a letter encouraging me. Many Christians "are hungry for a breakthrough," he said, "especially those faithful leaders in the churches who give so much of their time and energies in serving God. Sunday School teachers, deacons, pastors—they all cry out for more of the power of God in their churches and in their lives. All their activities have only made them tired! They need a breakthrough!"

You could probably make a list of breakthroughs you would like to see. So do it: make that list, then ask God to use these pages to speak to you in very practical, specific terms. Commit to listen and obey.

Lay down all your reasonings, excuses, hesitations, and fears, and let God teach you the truth He taught me so forcefully during those three August days: He is still in the business of breakthrough.

1

WHERE THERE'S A WALL,
THERE'S A WAY

*"I will go before you and make the rough places
smooth; I will shatter the doors of bronze, and
cut through their iron bars"
(Isa. 45:2 NASB).*

It started quietly, outside the Soviet Union, hundreds of miles from
Moscow, nearly two years before the coup. It is the classic story of
breakthrough—the tale of the first Communist domino to fall. An
official whose name no one remembers made an almost offhand
announcement. His words proved to be the hole that appeared just
before the dike gave way.

Hours later, the world watched, stunned, as a human flood poured
through the hole. It was midnight, November 9, 1989: the Berlin Wall
was down. Oh, the structure still stood; but the 28 miles of brick and
wire that had for 28 years mocked all challengers was defeated and over-
run. The wall had long painted the world's most graphic picture of
oppression. In its beginning, soldiers shot an 18-year-old East Berliner
trying to go over its top, and then watched him bleed to death at its foot.

Now the same wall depicted oppression's failure. For two days, soldiers watched throngs scale the wall, dance on top of it, chisel away
pieces of it, or drive honking through its gates. By proclamation of the
Communist government, East German citizens could, for the first time
in 37 years, leave their country without permission at any point along
its borders and return—or not return—at will.

Hundreds of thousands had already left during the first ten months of 1989. The multitudes who stayed gathered for peaceful mass protests. East German Communist leaders abruptly threw open the wall in a desperate attempt to keep their people and to keep a remnant of their party's power.

Leaders of the free world stammered out their delight. Even those best acquainted with global events were caught off guard by the decision. *Time* magazine reported, "Only a few weeks ago, East Germany seemed one of the most stolidly Stalinist of all Moscow's allies and the one least likely to undergo swift, dramatic change."[1]

U.S. News & World Report said the breakthrough occurred "in one bewildering instant, almost too fast for us to realize what happened." *U.S. News* also declared, "Not even a panzer thrust ever changed the political realities of Europe so swiftly."[2]

Meanwhile, in Berlin, a two-day celebration heralded the reunion of a city that had been divided for too long.

A World of Walls

All of us face walls—walls that separate us from the places we want to be, the persons we desire to become, the relationships we need to develop. Most frustrating to us as Christians are the walls that keep us from getting where we believe God intends us to be.

Our walls often seem impenetrable. Occasionally, we might make a run toward one of them—and even get close enough to peek over the top. But then, like that East German youth, we get shot down. We lie and bleed for a while and, though *we* don't die, hope does. Still bearing the scars of our wounds, we limp back to living in the wall's shadow.

Perhaps you face a wall in your relationships. A loved one has cut himself or herself off from you, or vice versa, and you see no way the two of you will ever again be close. A person with whom you have to deal stands, unyielding, against your every idea or effort.

Perhaps your unscalable wall is a recurring sin, an entrenched attitude, or a bad habit you cannot seem to conquer.

Perhaps impassable circumstances loom just ahead on the path you thought you were supposed to take. Maybe you keep running into an injustice, either against yourself or someone else, that refuses to be corrected.

Perhaps you're living behind the wall of thwarted goals. Try as you might, you can't get your head above water financially. You can't find the satisfying, paying job you badly need or want. You can't get your life organized, your quiet time regulated. You want to be slimmer, but can't get the weight off (and keep it off); or, already too thin, you want to eat right, but can't seem to stop dieting. You and your spouse can't have a child.

Or, your thwarted goals may not be for yourself, but for others. You long to see your husband take the spiritual lead in your family. You ache to see one you love turn (or return) to God. You want your church to break out of its rock-along rut and display God's power. You cry to see our country and our world caught up in true revival.

In one way or another, we all need to experience breakthrough, often in the physical realm, but even more so in the spiritual. We live in a world of walls: walls of severed relationships, entrenched sins, unjust circumstances, and thwarted goals. The world too cries for breakthrough.

A Way Through

Webster's Seventh New Collegiate Dictionary defines *breakthrough* as "1: an act or point of breaking through an obstruction. 2: an offensive thrust that penetrates and carries beyond a defensive line in warfare. 3: a sudden advance in knowledge or technique."

In the spiritual realm, as in the physical, breakthrough may carry any, or all, of those three connotations.

An Offensive Thrust

Through prayer and obedience, we who know Jesus Christ personally may make an offensive thrust that penetrates Satan's defensive line. My church, for instance, recently started a ministry to the hearing impaired. Due to one young woman's energy and sense of call, we are now reaching a group that no other church in our community was reaching.

The hearing-impaired youths and adults who attend our services have almost no previous exposure to the Christian faith. They live in the Bible Belt, but don't know even the most basic Bible stories and truths. Until now, Satan held them hostage in his territory because no believers tried to claim them.

Just weeks after the ministry began, a teenaged girl, Jolene, became our first convert. No one who saw her baptism will likely forget it. While she, our pastor, and the translator stood in the baptismal waters, Pastor Tommy asked Jolene, "Where is Jesus?"

She answered aloud, "In—my—heart!"

"Then, in obedience to the Great Commission of our Lord Jesus Christ and upon your open and unashamed confession of faith in Him, I now baptize you, my sister, Jolene . . ."

While he spoke, Jolene literally sobbed. He immersed her. Coming up from under the water, she gave a little jump for joy, grabbed Pastor Tommy around the neck, and hugged him.

Women and men all over the sanctuary wiped tears from their eyes. We had witnessed breakthrough.

A Sudden Advance

Breakthrough in the spiritual realm may also come as a sudden advance in knowledge or insight. Without warning, the Holy Spirit will open a Christian's eyes to see what, only moments before, could not be seen.

One who wrestles with a difficult problem and continues to lay it before the Lord and seek His wisdom will often, in a "breakthrough moment," understand exactly what needs to be done.

One who studies the Bible, not with a hit-or-miss or a skim-the-surface approach, but searching for buried treasure, will often find an unexpected and precious nugget. I had such an experience as I studied for a Sunday School lesson I was to teach. The passage for that particular Sunday, Isaiah 7, proved hard to understand and even harder to apply. Ahaz, an ungodly king of Judah, was about to be attacked by two enemy kings. God sent the prophet Isaiah to tell Ahaz, "Don't be afraid. The Lord is going to snuff out both those kings and their nations" (Isa. 7:4, author's paraphrase). Ahaz brushed off God's message, yet the Lord insisted on giving a sign that He was going to do as He had said. And in spite of Ahaz's failure to heed or obey Him, God brought about the promised deliverance.

For the life of me, I couldn't understand why God did all that for Ahaz—nor what lesson we were to learn from it. Did the incident imply that God gives us all assurance of victory, regardless of how we treat Him? I read and reread the passage. I poured over commentaries and other Bible study helps. I prayed.

About three days into my study, the Lord gave me precious insight: Ahaz became king when he was 20 years old. His father and grandfather before him had, for the most part, been godly rulers. The attack of the enemy kings came at the start of Ahaz's reign. God used the opportunity to offer Ahaz assurance of His power, His presence, and His protection. Almighty God went out of His way to give Ahaz a basis for believing in Him. Yet King Ahaz turned on his heels and walked away from everything God held out to him. The rest of his reign was marked by a downward spiral into sin and by constant defeat in battle.

The application was equally exciting. As I sat before a class of women the next Sunday morning I said, "God has gone even further out of His way to offer us assurance, to give us a basis for believing in Him. He faced death for us in the person of Jesus. Let's not do as Ahaz did. Let's heed the warning he ignored: 'If you do not stand firm in your faith, you will not stand at all'" (Isa. 7:9*b* NIV).

In refusing to back off from a hard passage of Scripture, I had experienced breakthrough.

An Act of Breaking Through

Sometimes, God "moves mountains" by barreling through the middle of them. He promised the ancient Persian ruler Cyrus, "I will go before you and make the rough places smooth; I will shatter the doors of bronze, and cut through their iron bars" (Isa. 45:2 NASB). God made that promise 150 years before Cyrus was born.

In time, God brought His promise to pass. He shattered unshatterable doors so that a pagan emperor could walk through. Then God used that pagan ruler to bring His people, the Jews, out of captivity. As our God demonstrated through Cyrus, no obstruction can keep Him from accomplishing His purposes.

Cindy saw God shatter some "doors of bronze" in her behalf too. Cindy had committed her life to missions in 1982 as a senior in high school, but obstacles kept blocking her path. Wanting to be a medical missionary, she enrolled in a college premed program. Her grades were not good enough to get her into med school.

At graduation time, she had the option of finishing with one major or going to school an extra year and completing three. Even though her best friend Shawn was graduating and heading out to spend two years doing missions work overseas, Cindy believed God wanted her to stay in school. She stayed.

Then in August 1987, just as she was beginning her fifth year of college, Cindy learned she had leukemia. The doctor who first discovered the disease told her, "If you make it the next three months, we will be surprised."

Shocked and frightened, Cindy was utterly confused as to what

God was doing. She still wanted with all her heart to tell God's good news to people outside the US. She asked, "Lord, why have You given me all these desires of my heart, and I've never accomplished any of them, and my life is almost over?"

Tired and sick, Cindy was also grieving over a series of deaths of persons she loved: the music and minister of youth under whom she had become a Christian in 1979, her father, and her grandmother. A month after Cindy found out she had leukemia, a college friend died while taking a chemotherapy treatment for the disease. Cindy found herself praying, "OK, Lord, if this is the plan, that's just great, because I want to give up."

But death was not God's plan for Cindy at that time. She began to respond to chemotherapy. In October 1987 she met and helped the missionary family with whom her friend Shawn had served. (Ron, Margie, and their three boys had to return to the US from Latin America because Ron had been diagnosed with lymphoma.) A year passed. Cindy had been in remission for some time. Ron, also in remission, took his family and returned to Latin America in December 1988.

The next July, Ron, Margie, and their boys returned to the States. Ron was sick again and was scheduled to undergo a bone marrow transplant. Cindy was certain what God wanted her to do. She quit her job in one city, moved to another city, and became mom to the three boys while Margie stayed with Ron in the hospital. Then, in November, Cindy found she too had relapsed. The family to whom she had ministered began to take care of her.

On first diagnosis, her blood count was not nearly as bad as it had been the first time she had leukemia. But this time, when Cindy began chemotherapy treatments, she started having complications. Her liver quit functioning properly; her spleen enlarged to three times its normal size; her blood platelet level dropped so low Cindy had to brush her teeth with a cotton swab. "Maybe a few more months," her doctor tried to encourage her.

By that time, it was May. Cindy had been fighting this second round with the disease for six months. Her missionary family was leaving the first of June for Latin America. Because of Margie's duties and the ages of the children, they needed someone to go teach the boys and help with other aspects of their ministry. Cindy longed to be that someone—but she could not.

Then, three days before Ron and Margie were to leave, Cindy

went in for a treatment. As she waited in the treatment room, already feeling physically sick because of what she knew she was about to endure, she heard the doctor in the hallway tell the nurse, "You need to get her blood checked again. You've got it mixed up with someone else's."

Three blood tests later, the doctor entered Cindy's room. He greeted her with the words, "You won't believe this. You are well."

Thrilled, Cindy told him, "See, God did this, because people all over have been praying for me."

Almost afraid to hope, she began wondering if she might now be able to join "her family" in Latin America. Big obstacles still stood in her way. During her second illness she had been uninsured, so she had a large debt. She needed insurance in order to go overseas; she saw no way of getting any. She also needed some means of financial support. Because she might come out of remission at any time, the mission board she had hoped would send her couldn't do so.

One by one, God bulldozed those obstacles, just as He had done with her illness. He provided money to pay her debts, primarily through gifts that appeared anonymously in her mailbox. He provided not one, but three, kinds of insurance—cancer, health, and life. Cindy's pride made her not want to try to raise her own support. However, believing strongly that God wanted her to do so, she sent 300 letters to people she knew, as well as to other people suggested by Christian friends. Within a month, she had raised 70 percent of her needed support for a year.

Cindy left for Latin America in August 1990. By the time she returned to the States for a checkup three months later, she had seen 52 people accept Christ.

She told friends at the time, "Maybe I will be sick again, and maybe I won't. I don't know that. Only the Lord knows that. But I know for now I want to use my time how He has planned for me.

"And I'm glad that, if those were the only three months I had, I was able to go." Cindy completed her year in Latin America, with all checkups showing her still clear of the leukemia. Then she returned to the States to work toward a degree in nursing—and further service overseas.

For Cindy, God's breakthrough in her behalf was overwhelming. Her life's dream and prayer had come true. As God plowed down obstacles to make that dream a reality, she saw His love in a way she never had before.

A God Who Opens the Way

As Christians, we can live in daily anticipation of breakthrough. We serve the God Who can shatter any obstacle, reveal any truth, and penetrate any enemy. He has, in fact, run roughshod over the ultimate enemy, death. Sadly, most believers have heard of the most amazing of all breakthroughs so often it fails to awe us anymore.

Turn your mind inside out and think of the old, old story from a new perspective. Picture death as a cave—a cave which all enter. On the far side of that cave lies a land of endless light and life, but no one can get to it, for the cave is inescapable. Oh, a few who've gone in have come out again. A man named Lazarus and a dead son or two were raised by God's grace, but they merely backed out the entrance, and they only stayed out for a time. Eventually, they reentered the cave, to stay forever.

Then came Jesus. As God, He could have lived eternally without facing death. Yet, He chose to be born—still God, yet man—knowing, agreeing, that one day He would have to enter the cave. When he was 33 years old, that day came.

Obviously, Jesus didn't die of old age; nor did He succumb to illness. He wasn't an accident victim. He walked to a Roman cross, allowed impotent human beings to raise Him up on it, and—for my sake and yours—entered death that way.

A few of Jesus' friends buried Him. They thought He was Messiah, but they knew the cave was inescapable. Yet, Jesus Christ, God in flesh, conquered death. In so doing, He opened the way to life for everyone who would follow Him. He fulfilled God's Old Testament promise:

"One who breaks open the way will go up before them;
they will break through the gate and go out.
Their king will pass through before them,
the Lord at their head" (Mic. 2:13 NIV).

Caution #1

The Lord of breakthrough goes before us. Yet, we can't trick Him into performing feats of breakthrough to tickle our fancies. He acts when He will in the ways He knows best. He is committed to breaking through only those obstacles that stand in the way of *His* purposes. God has stated His ultimate purpose clearly: "to bring all things in heaven and on earth together under one head, even Christ" (Eph. 1:10*b* NIV).

When He knocked down the Berlin Wall and other walls of communism, He didn't necessarily do so in order that people could flow out. He didn't delight in the drunken partying that took place while some East and West Germans celebrated. He wasn't issuing an invitation to those who'd lived long in poverty to get rich quick. Nor did He intend to recreate state churches that would oppress believers of other denominations.

Rather, His purposes in the happenings in Eastern Europe and the former Soviet Union line up with His character. In mercy, He accomplished breakthrough to alleviate suffering. In grace, He opened the way for the good news about Jesus to flow where it could not flow freely before.

The Apostle Paul knew God as the Lord of breakthrough. Soon after Paul entered Europe with the gospel, he and his companion Silas were thrown into a Philippian jail. That very night, God used an earthquake to break open the prison doors. Not only did Paul and Silas go free; a jailer found salvation.

Later, Paul was jailed in Jerusalem. The following night, the Lord appeared to Paul, but this time only to comfort, not to deliver. Still a prisoner, Paul was taken to the seaport city of Caesarea and basically ignored for two years. Then, because he asked to be tried before Caesar, he was carted off to Rome.

For years, the greatest first-century ambassador for Christ remained under arrest while the Lord seemingly worked no miraculous breakthroughs. Yet God was still accomplishing His purposes. For, even when he was in chains, Paul spread the good news wherever he went. During his imprisonment Paul wrote letters that form the bulk of our New Testament. According to Christian tradition, Paul was finally released from prison. Later, though, he was imprisoned again, and finally beheaded.

Why was breakthrough miraculous and immediate one time, yet slow to happen and accomplished by "natural" means the second time? Why did no breakthrough free Paul the third time he was jailed? Perhaps because God sometimes finds ways other than breakthrough to accomplish His purposes. Perhaps because breakthrough sometimes happens inwardly, rather than outwardly. Perhaps because God always works His breakthroughs in His way and His time.

If the breakthrough you're seeking doesn't line up with God's purposes, timing, and ways, don't expect Him to be a party to your efforts. But if, when you peek over that impenetrable wall, you see:

- growth in Christlikeness for yourself or someone else;
- salvation for one individual or many;
- unity in the church, the body of Christ;
- godly love demonstrated;
- injustice overruled;
- work done in God's power for His glory;
- the fulfilling of God's goals for your life, your church, your nation, your world;

you may well be on target in seeking breakthrough.

Caution #2

Breakthrough is often spectacular—but not always. In fact, if you're not watching, you may miss some miracles of breakthrough. One word sometimes translated *break through* in the Old Testament is, other times, rendered *hatch*. The latter rendering reminds us: breakthrough can happen quietly and by degrees.

A baby chick struggling to break through its shell expends much energy. It first makes a small crack, then more and larger ones, before finally creating the hole that frees it. It emerges, without noise or fanfare, from that shell. Only those watching are aware that breakthrough has occurred. The hatching of a new life is no less a miracle than the shattering of an impenetrable wall.

In the book *Transformed One Winter*, Marsha Spradlin tells of the months she lay in a hospital room a hair's breadth away from death. Doctors could not find the cause of her illness or any way of treating it. Finally, they allowed Marsha to go home because they could do nothing else for her. She had made no miraculous improvements. The miracle was the fact that she was alive.

After her release from the hospital, Marsha did improve, though her progress came painfully slowly. She began to spend a few hours a day outside her apartment. She started writing about her experiences and feelings. She began ministering to others. Finally, she returned to work. Though not cured, she found the disease in remission. Looking back later, Marsha could see how far she had come. She had experienced breakthrough—quietly and by degrees.

An Invitation to Cooperation

God doesn't intend that we break through every wall we find standing in our way. He intends some walls to turn us back. He gives strength to leap other walls, or wisdom to find an open way through.

However, when a wall stands between us and His purposes for us, and He shows us no other alternative, He means for us to go through it. He does not demand that we butt our heads against the stones till we're bloody and senseless. Nor does He require that we shoulder the immovable till we crumple.

He is the Lord of breakthrough. He is the "One who breaks open the way" before us. He wants to teach us how to cooperate with Him in bringing about breakthrough.

2

WHY SO FEW BREAKTHROUGHS?

"He that goeth forth and weepeth, bearing precious seed, shall doubtless come again with rejoicing, bringing his sheaves with him"
(Psalm 126:6 KJV).

"Want to go to Russia?"
The friend who asked me that question in August 1990 had no idea the impact it would have on my life.

"Yes!" I answered. But even a month earlier, I probably would have turned her down flat.

In 1984, my husband, Jerry, and I spent a free week in Rome, thanks to Holiday Inn Priority Club. A year later, I rocked our new baby girl while watching vivid TV reports of terrorist bombings in major European cities.

What if we'd won that trip *this* year, I thought, and we went. And Megan was here. And I ran into a terrorist bomb and didn't come back—and she had to grow up without a mother. I made the decision never to leave my child and travel overseas.

By 1989 Jerry and I had two daughters. I spent nights away from the girls on occasion but was still terrified at the idea of foreign travel. That year, God began to nudge me. "This is one area you haven't given to Me," He seemed to say.

I began to believe He wanted me to volunteer for short-term missions work . . . overseas. At first, I ignored Him. Then, I reminded

Him, "I can't go now, Lord. Jerry's employer is trying to relocate us. We haven't been able to sell the house. We don't know Your will about this move . . . whether or not we will go, or when we might be moving. I can't commit to a missions trip now."

The Lord continued to nudge. Finally I told Him, "All right. When we know where we're going to live, I'll apply for a foreign missions trip."

In July 1990, Jerry resigned the job that would have taken us to South Carolina and accepted a job that settled us for a time in Mississippi. The first of August, I mailed a card to a foreign missions board, stating my availability.

Before receiving a reply, I attended a Christian women's leadership conference in a nearby town. That's where my friend popped the question: "Want to go to Russia?"

At her words, my insides did a flip. "This is it," God seemed to say. "This is your trip."

My friend's trip was slated for August 1991. A group of young women called Enterprisers would be going to Moscow to distribute Bibles. I knew no other details when I sat on my bed a day or two later and casually asked Jerry, "Can I go to Russia?"

He snorted, "If you want to." His tone implied he couldn't imagine that I'd want to.

I prayed long and hard before sending in my application. Finally, God used the Scriptures to confirm the original stomach flip I'd felt. He was opening this door, and He wanted me to go through it.

On my application, I had to tell why I wanted to go to Moscow. My answer began, "I want to go because I'm afraid to go." I believed God was asking me to walk through fear, thus entering into a new dimension in my relationship to Him. By doing at His request what I was terrified of doing, I would be saying in unmistakable terms, "Lord Jesus, I love You."

If, on the other hand, I gave in to the fear, I felt I would become a slave to it. Both my spiritual growth and my relationship with my Lord would suffer.

I was still waiting to hear whether I'd been accepted for the Moscow Project—which had by then been changed to early September—when the Persian Gulf War broke out. In February, I received a letter from one of the trip leaders. It began:

"So much has happened in the world since I last wrote to you in January. These changes have slowed the process for nearly anyone planning to travel beyond our nation. And Russia has become a primary place of unrest."

My stomach knotted as I continued to read. The old fear rolled over me in waves. Once more, I could see myself leaving—and not coming back.

The letter outlined in detail the risks, the high costs, and the expected hardships of the proposed trip. Enclosed was a pink card I was to fill out and return. The card simply asked that I check one of the following:

- Please keep my application active for the Moscow Bible Project.
- Please remove my application from the active list for the Moscow Bible Project.

The only other information requested was name, phone, and date.

I carried that card around for ten days. In the meantime, I asked Jerry to read the letter and pray about it. I told him, "If you have any hesitations about my going, I'll decline."

While waiting for his response, I prayed too. Finally, I decided that if Jerry agreed, I would still apply to go. I had mixed emotions when he told me, "I think you ought to go ahead."

By divine arrangement, I was at that very time preparing to present a dramatic monologue on Esther. In the monologue, Esther stands at her window on the day she has agreed to go in to King Xerxes and plead for the lives of her people. She speaks to her cousin Mordecai, who cannot hear her, but whom she knows is sitting just outside the king's gate, waiting word of the outcome of her visit.

At the close of the monologue, Esther says, "It's time, Mordecai. I go in to the king, even though it is against the law. And if I perish, I perish" (Esther 4:16b NIV).

When I mailed in my pink card, I understood how Esther felt as she said to Mordecai, "I go." Of course, I knew Esther's story had a happy ending; but I also remembered a more recent story of others who had set out with Esther's attitude. In 1956 five young men had gone at God's call to take the gospel to Ecuador's savage Auca Indians. The Aucas murdered all five.

Six weeks after it began, the Persian Gulf War ended. Threatened terrorist bombing of international airports did not materialize. With that crisis past, I spent the spring and summer preparing for the trip.

Another change: the dates of September 1-8 were changed to September 2-10. Our itinerary broadened to include not only Moscow, but also the Soviet cities of Frunze (later renamed Bishkek) and Yalta.

Trip participants had to undergo training, plus other preparations and packing. I was hurtling toward our scheduled departure date, hoping to have everything done just in time, when news of the August 19 coup stopped me dead in my tracks.

Then, August 21, the coup crumbled. Evidence of God's hand in the whole affair was breathtaking. When official word came that the Enterprisers were going, I said, "Count me in."

Though I had no misgivings about my decision to make the trip, I savored every moment I spent with the girls. I gave them baths, saw my oldest off to her first week of first grade, played with my youngest, and kissed them both goodnight with special, almost sad, tenderness. God had told me to go, and I was thrilled to obey; but He still had not said what would happen when I went.

On Wednesday before leaving for the Soviet Union the next Monday, I discovered a verse from the Psalms that God used to speak directly to me: "He that goeth forth and weepeth, bearing precious seed, shall doubtless come again with rejoicing, bringing his sheaves with him" (Psalm 126:6 KJV).

I had already done a good bit of weeping: over the truths God had showed me as I prepared for the trip, over the spiritual needs of the Soviet peoples, over the amazing work of God in overthrowing the coup. I was going forth bearing the precious seed contained in thousands of Russian New Testaments.

I felt like doing a back flip! For the first time since my breakthrough of obedience more than a year earlier, God was assuring me: I would doubtless come again.

How God Approaches Breakthrough

We who traveled to the Soviet Union for the Moscow Project experienced astounding breakthroughs in connection with the trip. Looking back, I'm tempted to wonder: Why so many then, and at other times, so few? In fact, why do we who serve the Lord of breakthrough so seldom experience His breakthrough work? God is all-wise. Many times He chooses to work by other means. But I believe He sometimes desires to break through, yet does not. What restrains Him? What looses Him those times He does unleash His mighty breaking power?

To answer those questions, let's examine three approaches to breakthrough that God takes: Sometimes, He *promises* it. Other times, He *commands* it. Most often, He brings about breakthrough as a *result*.

When God Promises Breakthrough

Isaiah 35 describes a coming day of breakthrough. Like a winning football team ripping through the banner that proclaims them as winners, God will emerge both to avenge and to save. On that day the blind, deaf, lame, and dumb will see, hear, leap, and shout. Life-giving waters will spurt through the hard desert crust. These gushing waters will quench the thirst of the redeemed who travel the highway of holiness to Zion (see Isa. 35:8).

Isaiah never saw the ultimate fulfillment of that promise but he claimed it. He wrote the promise down for coming generations to read and claim until the time of its fulfillment.

Many of God's promises, like those in Isaiah 35, are not fulfilled immediately. In fact, God often brings His promises to pass only after a stretch of time in which their fulfillment seems impossible. If He is going to act immediately, He usually just *acts*, without announcing beforehand what He's going to do. He saves His promises for those times when faith will be required to hold to them. He offers them as "clinging points" when all else falls away.

I know a woman who believes God has given her a promise; He is going to give her husband victory over his temper. The husband, a believer, hasn't physically abused his family, but for years his fits of anger grew worse, not better. Finally, afraid of what his temper and her toleration of it were doing to the children, the wife put her foot down. She demonstrated the tough love that says, "We've gone the wrong way long enough."

The couple sought professional Christian help. The husband has made some strides forward, and a few back. My friend continues to cling to God's promise. I believe that she will see breakthrough.

Has God given you a promise of breakthrough? Have you long since boxed it and put it up on a back shelf? How many breakthroughs have you missed by giving up on God's promises too soon?

When God Commands Breakthrough

If ever a people needed a breakthrough, the Israelites did. They fled Egypt the night of the death angel's visit. At God's command, they camped at a seemingly foolish place. While the Red Sea lay before them, Pharaoh's forces approached rapidly from behind.

The people complained; Moses prayed; God gave Moses an order: "Lift up your staff and stretch out your hand over the sea and divide it" (Ex. 14:16a NASB).

"Now wait a minute," Moses might have said. "I can't divide the sea, and I'd look awfully foolish trying."

It did seem illogical. Instead of promising breakthrough, God had commanded it. His words might be translated, "Stretch out your hand over the sea and break through it."

No person can, with an outstretched stick, divide the waters of a sea. Moses could, however, take step number one: He could lift up his staff and stretch out his hand, just as God had said. When Moses took that step—when he risked looking foolish and accomplishing nothing, just because God had said do it—God took step number two for him. God divided the waters.

In my life, God commanded breakthrough when He commanded me to go overseas on a missions trip. I could not work out world conditions to make that trip possible, but I could apply for the trip and make preparations. When I stepped out in obedience to God's command, He accomplished for me what He required of me.

In some situations you face, God may say to you, "Walk into that brick wall and shatter it." Will you give Him the logical response? "Lord, if I walk into that wall, all I'll do is hurt my head!" Will you miss breakthrough because you consider the command to break through to be impossible? Or will you start walking?

When God Brings Breakthrough as a Result of Prayer

Samson had more strength than he knew how to handle. This Israelite went around devastating the lands of the enemy Philistines and slaughtering their mighty men. In fact, Samson had just killed 1,000 Philistines with the jawbone of a donkey when he found something he could not do: produce water to quench his great thirst.

How did Samson react? He cried out to God: "You gave me this great victory; am I now going to die of thirst and be captured by these heathen Philistines?" (Judg. 15:18b TEV).

Samson may have overstated his case; he probably was not *dying* of thirst. Still, he had a problem—and he prayed. He took the matter to the One Who could handle it. As a result, Samson experienced breakthrough: God split a hollow place so that water came out. Samson named the place Caller's Spring.

Prayers That Redirected a Life

Yun was born in China into a family of Buddhists. When he was 9, Yun moved with his family to South Korea. Then, at age 21, he left his wife and three children in South Korea while he came to the US to study. He planned to complete his education in 5 years, then return to Korea. In the States he made many friends, most of them Christians. He says, "They told me they were praying for my salvation, but I did not pay attention."

Two years after Yun moved to the US, the Korean War broke out. According to Yun, his wife and children "were scattered all over the country, trying to escape the war zone." He says, "I thought I had lost them. I never believed they could have survived."

For 2 years, Yun heard nothing. Then he learned that all four members of his family were alive. Still, he could not rejoin them, nor could they join him. Eight years passed. Finally, after exactly 10 years of separation, Yun's family was reunited with him in the States. During all this time Yun, medical arts department director of a university medical school, was not a Christian, but his Christian friends were praying.

Finally, breakthrough! Yun says, "The Holy Spirit revealed to me all the goodness which I had received, and truly did not deserve. I recognized that I was a sinner and repented to the Lord Jesus Christ for forgiveness. My wife and I accepted Jesus Christ as our personal Saviour and Lord. We dedicated our lives to obeying His words, trusting His promises and loving Him, being faithful servants without any condition or limitation." Yun began seeking the Lord's will for his life.

One day, he had an opportunity to board a Chinese ship docked in his city. He was thrilled. He had not had the chance to associate with any of his countrymen for 15 years. Assuming those to whom he talked were probably Christians too, he began sharing about his new life in Christ. As he talked, the puzzled men asked him, "Who is Jesus Christ?"

Yun left that ship distressed. He had not realized that many of his people have no idea Who Jesus is. Today, Yun works full time ministering to seamen and telling them of God's grace and love. He says, "I thank God for answering my friends' prayers."

Prayers that Propelled a Team

While 25 Enterprisers prepared for and took a 9-day trip to the Soviet Union, thousands of other people prayed.

Before the trip, nearly 3,000 women from across the US who attended two summer conferences promised us their prayer support. Thirty people made written commitments to be my prayer partners.

Many others told me they were praying. A whole college committed to pray for my roommate. Indeed, everyone who made the trip had prayer backing.

When news of the Soviet coup broke, those thousands who had already been praying for us thought immediately of our trip and redoubled their efforts. They carried us on their prayers to our destination and back.

When believers pray, breakthrough often results. How many times have you failed to see breakthrough because you've failed to call out to the Lord of breakthrough?

A Result of Purity

First Samuel 3:1 gives this sad commentary: "In those days . . . there were very few messages from the Lord, and visions from him were quite rare" (TEV). That last clause could read, "Visions were not breaking through."

In those days the boy Samuel served in the temple under the high priest Eli. Meanwhile, Eli and his sons were busy disgracing the priesthood. The sons lay with women who had come to the temple to worship. They also made a practice of syphoning off for themselves offerings the people brought to God. The son-priests despised their own father, as well as Almighty God—Eli let them get away with it all.

When Israel's God-called spiritual leaders led out in wickedness, the people followed suit. Before long, God's people lacked desperately needed breakthroughs. Why? Because they lacked desperately needed purity.

In his book *Against the Night*, Charles Colson contends, "We live in a new dark age. Having elevated the individual as the measure of all things, modern men and women are guided solely by their own dark passions; they have nothing above themselves to respect or obey, no principles to live or die for. Personal advancement, personal feeling, and personal autonomy are the only shrines at which they worship."[1]

To those who might argue that these comments apply not to the Christian community but to the non-Christian, Colson would point to George Gallup's description of US life today: "religion up, morality down." He reminds us that far from confronting impurity, today's church often encourages it. Much "Christian" preaching, for example, promotes not sacrifice, but self-interest; not spiritual growth, but an emotional high; not the quest for treasures in heaven, but the quest for material gain on earth.

I believe Colson's remarks hit dead center. The Christian church in America today, like the priesthood of Eli's day, is desperately impure. As a result, real revelations from God rarely break through.

We're certainly not clothed in righteousness when:

•We come to church, in varying degrees of regularity, but we're unmoved by pleas to abandon ourselves to Christ.

•We watch the TV shows and movies we want to watch, no matter how flagrantly they trample Christian values.

•We act around our nonchurchgoing friends exactly as they act. (After all, we don't want to seem dull or unfit to be one of the crowd.)

•We make lackadaisical efforts to do what God requires—efforts that do not refresh God, but rather repulse Him.

Some, like Colson, dare us to deal with our spiritual filthiness. But we American Christians have another problem that largely prevents us from doing what our prophets urge: we see what we want to see.

A certain mythical emperor had the same problem. You remember him. He loved clothes. As the story goes, two swindlers, pretending to be weavers, offered to make him a remarkably exquisite outfit. The outfit, they said, would be invisible to every person who was dull or unfit for his office. The emperor agreed.

Of course, the swindlers wove nothing. Yet, neither the emperor, nor any of his officials, nor any of the crowd before whom the emperor walked in solemn procession would admit that they could not see the clothes he was supposed to be wearing. Until a child said, "But he has nothing on."

A biblical church named Laodicea had the same problem. You might remember it. The Laodicean church liked finery. If anyone asked, and even before anyone asked, the church bragged, "I am rich; I have acquired wealth and do not need a thing."

Like the emperor, this church marched around naked, thinking itself remarkably well-clothed. Like him, it refused to see what unbiased eyes found obvious. Until one day the God Who came to earth as a child declared, "Church, you are wretched, pitiful, poor, blind, and naked." Translation: "But you have nothing on."

Do you see the alarming resemblance between wealthy, self-sufficient US Christianity, the fictitious ruler, and that historical church? Or—even more alarming—do you *not* see the resemblance?

We who make up today's church have become such products of our society that we often parade around spiritually naked, and don't even know it. Our pride blinds us to what ought to be obvious. As

Colson puts it, "They've grown so accustomed to the dark, they don't even realize the lights are out."[2]

The God Who longs to do mighty works among us offers us eye salve and white clothes. He alone can reveal to us our true state, and then cleanse us. When we reject His call to purity, we write the sad commentary No Breakthroughs across our lives and our land.

A Result of Obedience

The people of Isaiah's day were experiencing a long spiritual night . . . a night they wanted to end. Knowing that breakthrough often results from prayer, they had prayed and fasted. Yet God had not moved in their behalf. Confused and angry with Him, they asked why.

God answered, "For day after day they seek me out; they seem eager to know my ways, as if they were a nation that does what is right and has not forsaken the commands of its God" (Isa. 58:2 NIV).

Note the key words, *seem* and *as if*. The Israelites were using prayer not to seek God, but to try to manipulate Him. At the same time they were pleading with their Lord for breakthrough they were carrying on with disobedience as usual.

God told them, in essence, "Quit quarreling. Stop *mistreating* others and *treating* yourselves. Spend yourselves in behalf of others. Then, you'll see—daybreak."

A Series of Obediences

Faye and Paul experienced breakthrough as a result of a series of obediences. First, the two obeyed God by going to Nigeria in 1974 to live. There, they taught in a Christian school where most students were members of the Batonu tribe. Soon, they began to feel God's tug toward another tribe, the Fulanis. The largest nomadic people in the world, the Fulanis number between 10 and 14 million, and live in some 18 African countries. These cattle-raising people have traditionally moved often.

Today the Fulanis are a people in transition. Because of government restrictions and loss of cattle through disease, their nomadic lifestyle is dying. Still, the boys usually begin learning to herd cows at age four or five. The girls stay home and do domestic chores. Until recently, to be Fulani was to be Muslim, without exception. Although missionaries of various denominations have worked with the tribe since 1949, not one committed Fulani Christian surfaced for 30 years.

When Faye and Paul first became interested in the Fulanis, no one in their area was going to school. While continuing their work with the Batonu people, the couple began visiting nearby Fulani cattle camps, or *gaas*. For four years, they saw no converts; in fact, there was no real interest in the gospel. Faye sometimes wondered, *Is it possible to have any kind of breakthrough miracle with these nomadic people? How do you get a handle on a ministry with them?*

As she and Paul trekked from village to village, they wondered, *How would we ever bring together a church and grow a church? How would we ever convince the people to accept the Lord openly, though it might mean persecution? How would we ever plant a church building when the people are moving around?*

Then in 1980 a Batonu translation of the New Testament was completed. A Nigerian Christian sent Faye and Paul 100 copies of the New Testament to distribute as they thought best. They decided to present 1 New Testament to each of the 19 Batonu churches and 1 to each of the 80 Batonu villages in Nigeria. That would leave 1 extra New Testament.

As Faye, Paul, their son David, and several young Batonu pastors were returning home from presenting a Testament to the 80th village, they met a group of young Fulani herdsmen. The Fulani boys asked the Batonu pastors, "What are you doing?"

"We have been going from village to village giving people the book about God," came the reply.

"The what?"

"The book about God," the pastors said, and showed the Fulani youth the last New Testament.

"Please, may we have it, the last one you've got?" the Fulanis asked. "If it's a book about God, we'd like to have it."

"Why do you want it? You can't read. You've never been to school," the pastors reminded the boys.

"Please, we'd like to have it anyway. We want to show it to our chief."

After several minutes' discussion, the bearers of the remaining Batonu New Testament decided to give it to the youth. The Fulanis immediately took it to their Muslim chief. "What is it?" he asked.

"It's a book about God," they said. "That's what the white man told us, and he gave it to us."

"Well, what does it say?" the chief asked.

The youth answered, "We don't know. We can't read it. We don't know what it says."

"Well, go find out," the chief instructed.

The next Sunday, the chief sent 16 of his young men to the near-est church to find out what the book said about God. Sunday after Sunday, those young men returned. After a few months, several of them came forward, stating their desire to receive Jesus as Lord and Saviour.

Sometime later, 5 of the young men began meeting with Faye to learn to read. She had to teach them Batonu, because she didn't yet know Fulani. After six months, all 5 young men could read and write the Batonu language.

Prior to that point, none of the Fulanis who had professed faith in Christ had been baptized. In September 1982, 15 young men and 2 young women asked for baptism. They had already experienced perse-cution for their faith. Some were beaten; others had been abused ver-bally. Some of the young women to whom they were engaged were taken from them and offered to someone else for marriage. The 17 knew that baptism would bring the risk of greater persecution. They accepted that risk, and on September 26, all were baptized.

From that breakthrough, the first Fulani-speaking church in Nigeria was started. Then another . . . and another. By 1991, eight little Fulani congregations were meeting.

Several of those first 17 believers have gone on to pastor's school or Bible college and are now serving as pastors or chaplains. Others are lay pastors. Friends, relatives, and fellow villagers are receiving Christ. Many missionaries in Nigeria are now giving priority focus to Fulani work. They are seeking specific ways to meet the unique needs of the Fulanis, thus winning a hearing for the gospel of Jesus Christ.

No amount of prayer, purity, and obedience can force God to bring about breakthrough. Faye knows missionaries who have worked diligently with Fulanis in other countries for years and still have not broken through. They've developed friendships; they've planted the seed of the gospel; but they have yet to see any sign of harvest.

Obedience cannot force breakthrough. However, the break-throughs Faye and Paul experienced would never have happened apart from day-to-day obedience, persistence in spite of the lack of visible results.

As another missionary to a hard-to-reach people said, "When you fly in a plane over the sea, it can look so calm. But none of us are aware that below, the waters are moving. That's true with God too. We often assume He is not at work because we can't see anything, until all of a sudden something happens. And then we realize God has been working in the lives of people."

A Vessel of Breakthrough

Our God sometimes commands breakthrough. He sometimes promises breakthrough. Most often, He stands ready to send breakthrough on the heels of prayer, purity, and obedience. Why, then, do we experience so few breakthroughs? Too many of us who call ourselves Christians pray little, believe little, obey little, and sin much.

If you want to loose the Lord of breakthrough, let Him put His finger on the hindrances to breakthrough in your life. He may point out prayerlessness. He may rebuke a lack of faith. He may bring up sin you've not dealt with. He may indicate an area where you have balked instead of obeying.

Whatever He points out, be willing to see it as He sees it. Agree with what He says. Then, let Him cleanse you with the hot coals from the altar of the sacrifice of Jesus Christ.

Once purged, you can be a vessel of breakthrough.

3

SETTING THE STAGE FOR BREAKTHROUGH

*"The Lord has broken through my enemies before me
like the breakthrough of waters"
(2 Sam. 5:20b NASB).*

Twenty-four young women and 1 young man from 15 different states arrived in Birmingham, Alabama on August 31, 1991, with papers in hand. The papers included airline tickets; passports; visas to the Soviet cities of Moscow, Yalta, and Bishkek; orientation schedules; and trip itineraries. We each turned in one other paper soon after orientation began: the record of a completed training plan. Each plan included 50-plus hours of preparation required for Enterprisers to participate in the Soviet Union trip. Requirements fell into six categories:
- Bible study
- training in personal witnessing
- ministry/witnessing projects
- spiritual development
- cross-cultural training
- missions history

On our sheets, we listed preparations completed in each category and the date of completion. To ready myself for the trip, I had done five months of intensive Bible study on the subject "Called." I included missions praying in my daily quiet time. A friend and I weekly visited unchurched women in our community. During a local fair, I worked at a booth that offered a cup of water, a shady place to sit, and free Christian tracts and Bibles to passersby. I had studied missions history,

kept up with current events in the Soviet Union, read a book that
focused on the Holy Spirit's empowering, worked through a spiritual
growth journal, and completed a six-week study in witnessing.

At a Birmingham motel, the 25 of us gathered for a two-day orientation. These sessions would give us further insight into the culture
of the people among whom we would be working and force us to prepare ahead for situations we might meet. Even before orientation started, we began to realize the value of all those months of training.
Enterprisers team leader Andrea announced that due to a mix-up, the
trip that was supposed to take us from Birmingham to Pittsburgh to
New York to Helsinki to Moscow would now include another stop:
Leningrad. We had no visas for Leningrad, but were assured special
passes would be provided.

The stop in Leningrad would complicate our travel. Instead of
checking our bags to Moscow, we would check them to Leningrad,
retrieve them and take them through customs there, load onto buses,
ride from the international airport to a nearby national airport,
recheck our luggage, and wait for our Moscow flight. Going to
Leningrad meant adding another 6 hours to an already lengthy trip.
Instead of 17 hours, the journey would take 23.

On hearing the news, none of us had a party; but nobody got bent
out of shape either. We had been drilled on the importance of being
flexible as we went. Our prayer partners had joined us in praying that
we would be filled with God's Spirit throughout the trip. Thus prepared, we took the first challenge in stride.

Then the Enterprisers began to meet one another. Soon we found
that each of us had faced challenges in preparation for this trip to the
Soviet Union; the Leningrad challenge was not the first for anyone.

We found out reasons, other than the coup, that some of us might
have chosen not to go. Jamie and her family, for example, were pursuing appointment as career missionaries. If all went well, they would be
leaving in just a few months to devote their lives to missions work in
French-speaking West Africa. With that very real possibility before
her, Jamie might well have chosen to guard every minute of her
remaining time with family and friends in the States. Instead, she
chose to spend 11 days traveling to reach and minister to people with
a culture and language totally different from what she might soon have
to learn.

Because of family crises, Sheri had almost given her place on the
team to someone else. Her father had been in the hospital on three

occasions earlier in the year. Then, her brother had been hospitalized for six weeks after a motorcycle accident. The Tuesday before orientation began on Saturday, her ten-year-old niece, diagnosed with cancer, had a leg amputation. Sheri decided to take the trip only after her niece urged her to go on.

Linda is a diabetic. Tackling the strenuous travel schedule meant taking a very real physical risk. Linda had to bring all her shot paraphernalia, declare the medications she carried, and guard her sleeping and eating habits carefully.

Dan, the token male on our team, came at his wife Janet's urging. He had long wanted to visit Russia, and had even studied Russian in college. During orientation, Dan told us that the day we arrived in Moscow, Janet would undergo a hysterectomy. She was going ahead with the surgery—and he was going ahead with the trip—knowing they would be half a world apart when she was wheeled out of the operating room. Because of the unpredictability of the Soviet phone system, Dan didn't even know if he would be able to contact home to find out how the operation went.

Many of us were leaving behind young children. Wendy waved good-bye to four boys. Karon had no children yet, but she had just found out she was six weeks pregnant.

Amazingly, all those originally accepted for the Enterprisers team early in March made it to orientation that last day of August. Plus, we all made it to the Birmingham airport Monday morning, September 2. One young woman, Rebecca, arrived in tears. She had discovered late the night before that she had no ticket for one leg of the trip. By phone, she had been told that she would have a seat on the flight; but at the airport, she learned she did not have a seat.

While airline personnel found Rebecca a seat that did not exist, 10 Enterprisers were accepting a further schedule change. Leaving Pittsburgh, they would take a different flight from the rest of us, making an extra stop in Philadelphia. Those 10 had the pleasure of traveling from Philadelphia to New York on a bumpy commuter flight that made several of them airsick.

The other 15 of us had an interesting experience after boarding our plane in Pittsburgh. The jet found its spot in a long line of airplanes taxiing for takeoff at about the same time. We crawled and stopped, crawled and stopped, down the taxiway. Then, when we had almost reached takeoff position, our pilot came over the intercom to inform us, "Somebody doesn't like us. We've been pulled from the lineup because of our international connections' departure times. We'll be holding here a few more minutes."

It seemed spiritual enemy forces were set at every turn to hinder our going. Immediately, several in our group began to pray. I was in the middle of my silent petition when the pilot came back on the intercom: "Well, somebody *does* like us! We're going now!"

As it was, we touched down in New York at almost the exact time as the group coming by way of Philadelphia. We all ran through the terminal, boarded a bus to another terminal, and hustled through the ticket line there. (All our tickets had to be changed because of our new Leningrad destination.) We barely made the flight to Helsinki. We might not have made it had we been bumped on the taxiway in Pittsburgh.

We had an uneventful, but sleepless, overnight flight to Helsinki. On board, we met the 34 other men and women who would be teaming up with us to distribute Bibles in Moscow, Yalta, and Bishkek.

Tuesday morning at the Helsinki airport we hit another snag. The "special passes" to Leningrad we'd been promised had not materialized. Lamont, head of the combined teams, announced he was going downstairs to talk to the "powers that be." He said, "The worst that could happen is that in Leningrad they would send us back here."

He tried to reassure us that we wouldn't end up in some Soviet prison, but his words didn't comfort. In fact, something inside me said no. I believe it was God's Spirit telling me, "You've flexed as far as I want you to flex. Now it's time to stand." The Enterprisers stood in a large circle in the Helsinki airport that Tuesday morning and prayed. We asked God to quash any further delay and to move us through Leningrad to Moscow. God did.

Tuesday night, we stood in Red Square in the heart of Moscow, watching young Soviet cadets in carefully metered step carry out the changing of the guard at Lenin's tomb. Wednesday through Friday we were supposed to distribute Russian New Testaments in connection with Moscow's International Book Fair. Instead, Wednesday morning we learned that rumors we had heard were true: the book fair had been canceled.

Lamont told us, "I've already been talking with some of the Russian Baptist leaders. God is going to provide us other opportunities to distribute those Bibles."

That morning we visited the largest Baptist church in Moscow where we had a short service with a few of the Russian believers.

Then, we were supposed to load 14,000 New Testaments into our two tour buses, head out to two different places, and begin distributing the Bibles. Instead, we stood around inside the church after the service and talked for what seemed like hours. We later learned the paperwork for releasing the Bibles had taken much longer than expected.

By the time we got the Testaments loaded, it was almost lunchtime. Although a prepared meal was waiting for us at the hotel, our tour guides took each bus to a different souvenir shop and let us all out. Along the way, they named all the tourist attractions we would visit over the next two days.

It was now Wednesday noon; we began our trip early Monday morning. We still had 14,000 Bibles to distribute in Moscow before flying to other cities on Friday. We had not yet begun what we set out to do, and the tour guides' plans didn't seem to leave any time to do it.

I heard Lamont telling one of the guides, "These people are not ordinary tourists. They haven't come here to see the sights. They have come here to minister to the Russian people. You must let *us* set the schedule."

On the bus again, traveling back to the Cosmos Hotel for lunch, I prayed, Lord of breakthrough, loose us to do what we have come here to do!

Prepare First

Isaiah 54:2-3 calls those who want to experience breakthrough to make preparations for it: "Enlarge the place of your tent, stretch your tent curtains wide, do not hold back; lengthen your cords, strengthen your stakes. For you will spread out [or, *break through*] to the right and to the left" (NIV).

These words were written to the barren nation Israel. To them, God said, "Enlarge, stretch, lengthen, strengthen—you make the preparations first. The breakthrough will follow." The Lord gives similar instructions to His people today. Too often, however, we want to do it the other way. A real breakthrough seems so impossible in a given situation that to prepare for it seems only to ask to be disappointed. *If* the breakthrough comes, we decide, *then* we'll do what needs to be done to accommodate it.

Our missions trip team tried preparing for breakthrough God's way and found it works. King David did too. After many years of fleeing from King Saul and more years of reigning over only two of Israel's tribes, David was finally crowned king of all Israel. Immediately an enemy nation, Philistia, went into action. They mustered their entire army and set out to capture David.

Hearing what the Philistines were plotting, David headed for "the stronghold," most probably the cave of Adullam, the place where he hid for years from Saul. There, "David asked the Lord, 'Shall I attack the Philistines? Will you give me the victory?'" (2 Sam. 5:19 TEV). "Yes, and yes," the Lord answered.

So David attacked that mighty Philistine army and defeated them. After the victory, David declared, "The Lord has broken through my enemies before me like the breakthrough of waters" (2 Sam. 5:20*b* NASB). He named the place *Baal Perazim*, which means "Lord of breakthrough."

From David, we can glean at least six tips on setting the stage for breakthrough in our own lives.

Recognize the Need
While the Philistines gathered their troops, somebody alerted David to the potential danger. The Bible says, "David heard of it" (2 Sam. 5:17 KJV).

Is an area in your life, or in lives of those you touch, crying out for breakthrough? Have you "heard of," or recognized, the need? Or, are you unaware that you stand at a place where God wants to reveal Himself as the Lord of breakthrough?

Maybe you've gotten in a rut so deep you don't see the rut anymore. Maybe you cannot or will not admit how bad a situation is. Maybe you're looking at things as they appear outwardly and not viewing them from God's perspective. If you want breakthrough, you must see the need for breakthrough.

Larry arrived in Mubi, Nigeria, in 1982. His job: to start and grow churches in the area. He recalls, "When we first arrived in Mubi, we had 41 churches in one association. They had not started a new church in over ten years. The churches were plateaued and stagnant."

Over the next three-and-one-half years, Larry helped get 7 new churches started. Then, after a furlough in the States, he returned to find that the Nigerian churches had continued to start churches in his absence. "Still," he says, "my colleague Wiley and I were concerned." Though progress was being made, the two men felt very strongly that it was not enough.

As they prayed and talked, God gave them an idea. "We had a reservoir of young men who had grown up in our churches," he explains. "Many of them had even committed themselves to the pas-torate, feeling they were called of God to preach, but for various rea-sons weren't able to get into theological training." Larry and Wiley decided to hire these young men to work as full-time church planters for at least six months with a maximum of two years.

Under the program, each young man stays in one area three to six months witnessing to people, leading them to Christ, perhaps setting up literacy classes and training a team of leaders for the new church. Then he moves on, leaving the church to grow with lay leadership until it can call a full-time pastor.

Larry and Wiley called the plan Volunteer Apprentice Church Planter Program. In the first three years of the program, Larry worked with 15 young men who started 13 new churches. In Wiley's first four years, the young men with whom he worked started more than 40 churches. Many of the young men are now in theological training, preparing for the pastorate and continuing to plant congregations.

Larry says, "The breakthrough we experienced was in getting the churches to reach out and open new work by using these young church planters." If Larry and Wiley had not seen the need for life and growth, the breakthrough might not have happened. The plateaued and stagnant churches might have remained plateaued and stagnant. After the two men started a few churches themselves, they might have felt enough progress was being made. They might have missed the truth that breakthrough still was needed.

To begin preparing for breakthrough, ask God for eyes to see the places where He wants to do a breakthrough work. Then, take a fresh look at yourself, your family, your work, your church, your community, and your world. Make a mental note of barriers in any of these areas that stand in the way of His purposes.

Get Desperate

When David heard the Philistines were out to get him, "he went down to the stronghold" (2 Sam. 5:17 NASB). The stronghold was the place where David resorted when he knew he couldn't cope. He didn't with-draw there, never to be heard from again. He didn't go to give up. He retreated to a fortified place to prepare for the battle that lay ahead.

Imagine David in that cave. Perhaps he recalled the years he'd spent there hiding from Saul. Perhaps he felt again the fear, the loneli-ness, the depression of life as a fugitive. Perhaps he thought of the past seven years when he had ruled two tribes in Israel. During those years, he had not had to visit the cave. Maybe God used David's memories to intensify his desire to end forever the hiding and skirmishing. David yearned to go out boldly against the Philistines and win decisive victory. Before long, he who ran to the stronghold and waited there . . . *craved* breakthrough.

Once you recognize a need for breakthrough, how do you handle it? Do you charge headlong into the fray, yelling as you go for God to bless you with protection and victory? Do you retreat into despair, confident that, as badly as breakthrough is needed, it can never happen to you?

Rather than choosing either of those alternatives, why not do as David did? Let overwhelming need drive you to the stronghold. Run headlong to the Lord, admitting to Him that you cannot cope, while acknowledging that He can. There in God's presence, do as David urged himself to do: wait in silence. Confess, "For my hope is from Him. He only is my rock and my salvation, my stronghold; I shall not be shaken" (Psalm 62:5b-6 NASB).

In the areas where you know there is a *need* for breakthrough, stay before God until you *crave* breakthrough.

On the Heels of Desperation

Several years ago, when I first started to begin to recognize areas needing breakthrough in my own life, God brought my time problem to my attention.

I had two preschoolers, and I dreaded trying to go anywhere with them; I just could not seem to get us all together and out the door on time. Invariably, I would find myself yelling at them, or being late, or both. We'd had the problem a while. But as I faced the need, God increased my desire to see breakthrough in it. I grew more and more desperate to see Him act.

When I was desperate enough, He showed me several simple, but vital, steps to take. I began to:

•Start getting ready to leave *earlier* than I thought necessary. I had never allowed time for the accidents and holdups that invariably happened.

•Set a time to leave the house that would allow us to arrive five minutes early, and keep that "departure" time in mind as we prepared to go.

•Commit not to get angry, regardless.

•Keep the matter a prayer concern before God.

I still run late, but I've made monumental strides in the right direction. The breakthrough came on the heels of my own desperation.

Pray for Breakthrough

Once in the stronghold, "David inquired of the Lord" (2 Sam. 5:19 NASB). He asked God two questions:

"What do You want *me* to do, Lord?"

"What do *You* want to do?"

Like David, you cannot adequately prepare for breakthrough without praying for it. In some areas, you may realize that matters you've thought about, worried about, and talked about, you've not really prayed about. Maybe you've prayed, but only sporadically.

In those cases, make consistent, fervent, specific prayer your goal. Write down your requests. Keep them where you will remember to look at them and uplift them often to the Lord.

Regarding other situations, you may have prayed long and hard, without any apparent answer to them. In those cases, take time to reflect on how you've been praying. Ask God to teach you to pray more effectively.

As you consider your previous prayers about the matter, you may find you've never asked God either of the questions David asked. You may have prayed, "Do something, Lord," but never queried, "What do You want me to do?" You may have pleaded, "Do such and so . . . if it be Thy will," but never ventured, "What is Your will? What do You want to do?"

For too many years I shied away from asking God "what" questions because I didn't know He could answer them in a way I would understand. When David questioned God, the Lord answered in words, perhaps audible words. I know God rarely speaks audibly today. He's never spoken to me that way. I thought I had to pray, "if it be Your will" and then I'd know it *was* His will if He did it.

I've learned, however, that God can and often does reveal His will to His people before He acts. He delights in showing us His plans for at least two reasons: so we can cooperate in carrying them out, and so He can receive the glory for bringing them to pass.

No, He doesn't usually speak audibly; but He does speak clearly. He doesn't speak to our natural ears; He speaks to our spiritual ears. Hearing Him isn't as hard as it seems. Any Christian can do it—that is, any Christian who practices listening and who decides ahead of time to obey whatever he or she hears.

Years ago, the church I attended experienced a crisis. Sunday after Sunday I sat in the choir loft, watching dull eyes and lined faces remain unchanged throughout each worship service. We had a pastor, yet we were "distressed and downcast like sheep without a shepherd" (Matt. 9:36b NASB).

As I poured out my concern to God, He led me to a scriptural prayer: "May the Lord, the God of the spirits of all flesh, appoint a man over the congregation, who will go out and come in before them, and who will lead them out and bring them in, that the congregation of the Lord may not be like sheep which have no shepherd" (Num. 27:16-17 NASB).

Months later, God used the Scriptures again to tell me that what I was praying for was as good as done: "The Lord has sought out for Himself a man after His own heart, and the Lord has appointed him as ruler over His people" (1 Sam. 13:14 NASB).

At the time God spoke to me through that verse, nothing had changed outwardly. I kept praying anyway, confessing that He would do as He had said. Then, breakthrough! A change of pastors and a mighty outpouring of God's Spirit in and through our church.

Before you ask God, "What do You want *me* to do?" be ready to do whatever He says. You'll be surprised at the many different ways He can communicate to you exactly what steps He wants you to take.

Once you pray, "What do *You* want to do?" be alert for His answer. Listen for His voice as you study your Bible, attend a worship service, read a Christian book, talk to a friend or family member. Tell God you're practicing listening with your spiritual ears, and ask Him to help you hear. Then, rejoice when He answers and you know what He has said.

Get in on God's Plan

God told David not only what He intended to do but also how He intended to do it. David was to engage in a frontal attack, and God would hand the Philistines over to him. The breakthrough would happen "like a flood."

At other times in David's life, God had other plans. After David's first victory over the Philistines, for example, God called him to take action again, but a different kind of action. The Philistines had rallied. A vast army was preparing for another attack.

King David didn't make the mistake we often make; he didn't assume God would have the same battle plan the second time around.

Instead he asked, and God told him to take another route to break-through: "Do not go straight up, but circle around behind them and attack them in front of the balsam trees" (2 Sam. 5:23 NIV).

David got in on God's plan and was victorious again.

God's Plans for Jerome

Like Israel's ancient king, Jerome experienced breakthrough as a result of getting in on God's plan. When Jerome graduated from college with a master's degree in agriculture, he had his own plans. He would not pursue a higher degree because that would involve taking a foreign language. Jerome had no intention of tackling any language other than English. He would live the rest of his life with his wife, Joann, doing agricultural work in his home state of Georgia.

But when Jerome was 30, God confronted him with a verse designed to hit an agriculturalist right between the eyes. "I am telling you the truth: a grain of wheat remains no more than a single grain unless it is dropped into the ground and dies. If it does die, then it pro-duces many grains" (John 12:24 TEV). Jerome knew God was saying, "Die to your own plans and get in on Mine." Jerome did.

As a result, he and Joann soon found themselves living in Togo, West Africa, a French-speaking country. Later, God led the couple to a very undeveloped section of Togo called the East Mono area. There, the Lord further revealed His plans to Jerome, and Jerome began to carry them out.

During a three-and-one-half-year period, Christians from North Carolina and from Togo worked with the Ifé people of East Mono. Together, they drilled 130 wells and built 21 ponds, two bridges, a pharmacy, and an agricultural center. As a result, 50 churches and preaching points now stand in an area where before there were none.

In the early stages of the project that changed so many lives, Jerome's friend, former President Jimmy Carter, heard about it. President Carter asked, "Jerome, can you build a bridge?"

Jerome answered, "No, Jimmy, but God knows people who can. He's providing for those people to have the correct training and to come to Togo, and we're going to build those bridges."

You know what? God did it just that way because that's how He planned it—and because a man named Jerome, and many more Christians who had not previously thought God would ever send them so far from home, got in on God's plan.

If you're sensing the need for breakthrough in a certain area, if you're longing to see it happen, and if you believe God wants to bring it about, pray to understand not only *what* He wants to do but also *how* He wants to do it. Then listen for His go-ahead and for His step-by-step instructions.

Follow Through

David didn't make a move until he heard from God; then he did as God instructed. When God said, "Go up," David charged straight ahead. When God said, "Circle around," David attacked from the rear.

The Bible warns, "So then, the person who does not do the good he knows he should do is guilty of sin" (James 4:17 TEV).

You may know God wants you to confront a family member who has long chosen a path destructive to himself or herself and to the entire family. You may understand that you will have to exercise both love and uncompromising firmness. Will you do it?

You may know God wants you to speak out about a moral issue in which you long to see breakthrough. God may want you to write letters to government leaders or other influential persons. He may want you to speak to local groups or in some other way take a visible stand. Will you do it?

You may know God wants you to find a "yokefellow" to hold you accountable to stop a bad habit, to start a good one, or to stay on course in an area where you tend to get sidetracked. You even believe you know whom God wants you to approach. Will you do it?

Whatever the area, you've yearned for and prayed for breakthrough. You believe you know the first step God wants you to take. Will you take it? In all likelihood, He will guide you no further until you do. He rarely maps out an entire journey for His children, but most often reveals His plans one step at a time. That way, He ensures that you keep your eyes not on the map, but on Him.

If you balk, He waits. If you follow through, He breaks through. If you want to see breakthrough, do what He says.

Give God the Glory

In his first victory over the Philistines, David trounced the enemy that posed the biggest threat to his kingship. Forgetting all that had gone before, he could have claimed the victory and the glory as his own. Instead, David made sure the glory rested on the One Who deserved it. He announced, "*The Lord* has broken through my enemies" (author's italics).

If David had patted himself on the back for that first break-through, he would have cut himself off from later ones. Almighty God declares, "I will not give My glory to another" (Isa. 42:8b NASB). If David had tried to steal God's glory after the first battle with the Philistines, the second battle most probably would have had a far different ending.

"God Was Doing It"

Vince knows how important it is to respond to every breakthrough by giving God the glory. Born and raised in "a very rough blue-collar," multiethnic area of Chester, Pennsylvania, Vince says, "Although my mom was Roman Catholic and my dad was Italian Presbyterian, I didn't have much of a church background."

During the Vietnam era, Vince traveled with a navy show band called the Helmsmen. These travels took him around the world and introduced him to many cultures. In 1970, soon after his arrival in Seattle, Washington, a sailor led Vince to Christ. The sailor, who also discipled Vince, insisted that Vince memorize two Bible verses a week, share his faith spontaneously, and take part in small group Bible study. Vince says, "Two years later, while in Saskatoon, Canada, the Lord showed me in my quiet times what biblical baptism was all about." That summer, he was baptized.

While attending the University of Washington, Vince met and later married a girl who had "big, pretty blue eyes and a big heart for God." After college, Vince moved south to attend seminary, then for four years pastored a multiracial, inner-city church in Seattle. He describes the experience as "wonderful and difficult. We filled the building." Eventually, the thriving church moved to a larger building given to them by a disbanding sister church.

Since 1983, Vince has been involved in the Puget Sound area in ministry to people who speak a first language other than English. He describes the area as "very multiethnic, multicultural, and New Age/cult-impacted."

He says, "Our Lord has literally taken me from the East where I was raised, to the West where I was saved, to the North where I was baptized, to the South where I was educated. I married a girl from the Northwest with Lebanese heritage, and we serve the Lord doing foreign missions work on home mission soil! Isn't God good!"

By 1991, Vince had experienced an entire string of break-throughs. Every 4 months for the previous 96 months, a new Christian "language" congregation had started in the Puget Sound area; but Vince does not brag on himself. He says, "Recently, someone asked me what strategy I use. I was not able to point to any strategy except for the fact that God was doing it and I was simply making myself available to be a part of what God was already doing." He continues to remind himself and others that no one can take credit for what God alone can do.

Think back to a breakthrough you've experienced. Did you recognize God as the One Who brought it about? Did you tell the Lord and others that the credit belonged to Him? Or somewhere along the way, have you taken the credit for a breakthrough? Have you let others assume *you* did it? Have you cut yourself off from God's breakthrough work because, once upon a time, you stole His glory?

Breakthrough Will Follow

That September 1991, recognizing the Muscovites' great need for the Testaments we brought, and desperate to see those Bibles reach the ones for whom God intended, I prayed for breakthrough. Other members of our team and thousands back in the States were also praying. What happened as a result, only God could have done.

On Wednesday afternoon, September 4, half the team members boarded a bus and took New Testaments and Christian love to people in a psychiatric hospital and an alcohol rehabilitation center. At the rehab center, the group held an evangelistic service. About 150 men received Jesus Christ as Lord.

The other team members boarded a second bus bound for Red Square. In the shadow of beautiful St. Basil's Cathedral, perhaps the most well known of all Moscow landmarks, we held an evangelistic service. Afterwards, we handed out hundreds of New Testaments to people who were thrilled to receive them.

Later that afternoon we went to Arbat Street, a famous pedestrian street where artists and craftsmen display and sell their work. Again, we placed Bibles in hundreds of outstretched hands. Michael, a young artist, grabbed the New Testament I handed him. In broken English he exclaimed, "I am a believer. But no Bible. I pray for a Bible. But no money. Now I have a Bible!" Then, he kissed me four times on the cheeks.

Between Wednesday afternoon and Thursday night, we handed out all 14,000 Bibles in half a dozen street locations and three institutions in Moscow. Everywhere people flocked to get what we offered.

To have a copy of the Scriptures, drivers jumped out of cars at red lights, sophisticated businessmen made pedestrian U-turns, people in lab coats left their posts in a medical building. Some who received Bibles kissed them or clutched them to their chests. Some kissed the hands or cheeks of the givers. Others asked team members to sign their New Testaments. "Thank you," they said over and over in Russian. As I handed out each Testament, I tried to make eye contact with the person receiving it and to say in Russian, "Jesus Christ loves you." Time after time, I watched hard eyes melt into soft hope.

Looking back, I marvel at what God did through 59 people in such a short time in Moscow. And I rejoice that we, and the many believers who were praying for us, cooperated with Him over many months to set the stage for breakthrough.

4

WAITING

*"So then, my dear brothers, stand firm and steady.
Keep busy always in your work for the Lord, since
you know that nothing you do in the Lord's service
is ever useless"*
(1 Cor. 15:58 TEV).

Travel in the Soviet Union, while it was still the Soviet Union, could present quite a logistical problem. When 33 of our 59 member missions team traveled from Moscow to Yalta, we learned that truth from experience.

Yalta lies in the Ukraine. In December 1991 the USSR officially completed its split into three sovereign nations and 12 cooperating entities known collectively as the Commonwealth of Independent States. Until that time, the Ukraine was "the breadbasket of the Soviet Union." At the tip of a peninsula called the Crimea, jutting out into the Black Sea, is Yalta. In 1945 at Livadia Palace, just outside Yalta, Joseph Stalin, Winston Churchill, and Franklin D. Roosevelt held the famous Yalta Conference. The palace is still a major tourist attraction.

Mountains to the north protect Yalta from the bitter temperatures common to most of the Commonwealth's states. As a result, Yalta has become quite a popular resort. We were told, in fact, that the city's population of about 80,000 triples during the summer months. Gorbachev was vacationing there in mid-August (before we were there in September) when he was taken into custody by coup leaders.

Our flight out of Moscow was not scheduled to depart until 3:30 on Friday afternoon, September 6, so the 33 of us toured the Kremlin in the morning, ate lunch at the Cosmos Hotel, then piled into our bus for the ride to the airport. We knew we wouldn't be flying into Yalta. After our Aeroflot plane took us to another Crimean city named Simferopol, we would travel by bus the 25 miles from Simferopol to Yalta.

What we didn't know until we were on our way to the Moscow airport was that the 25-mile drive from Simferopol to Yalta takes two hours. The road is winding; the altitude high. Much of the way, the bus would have to work to go 25 or 30 miles an hour. Apparently, our itinerary planners hadn't known about the long drive either. Though we were scheduled to have supper that night at 7:00 with pastors from all over the Crimea, we wouldn't actually reach Yalta until 9:00.

Feeling the rub of an already upset schedule, we arrived at one of Moscow's national airports. Those of us hardy enough (and desperate enough before a two-and-one-half hour flight on an airplane without toilet facilities) used the holes in the floor in the women's bathroom. Then we congregated in an already full waiting area. The seats were all taken, so we stood. While we waited, our tour guide, Alla, took our tickets and went to check us in.

Finally, word came for us to line up to go through the security check. Word also came down the line to pray. No details. Just a word: Pray.

So, silently, we prayed: Lord, whatever is the problem, You can handle it. Please do.

We made it past the fierce-looking female security guard. We boarded the aging bus that would carry us out to the Simferopol-bound plane. Hoisting myself and my carry-on bag up onto the bus, I heard Alla explaining the problem to Alfred, our Yalta team leader. "The flight is overbooked by two," she said. "We may all get on, or two of us may have to wait for the next flight."

As word of the possible dilemma spread, we fought alarm and prayed harder. No one wanted to be left behind. Each of us imagined the nightmare of staying at the dirty airport overnight, then trying to communicate well enough in Russian to make the next flight to Simferopol, and somehow get from there over the mountains to Yalta.

The bus stopped beside the monstrous Aeroflot jet. A group of about 30 people stood at the foot of the plane. My first thought was, Those folks have just gotten off another bus and are about to board.

I soon realized no one was boarding. Instead, the people stood almost like statues. One young man who had apparently delegated himself spokesman had ventured halfway up the steps. He argued in Russian with two sturdy female flight attendants.

Piling off the bus, we stood beside and behind the people already there. Alla moved past us and joined the three standing on the stairs. She, the man, and the flight attendants had a lively debate that followed a pattern. The man would speak in sharp, staccato sentences. One attendant would flip briskly through a stack of papers she held in one hand. She would shake the papers in the man's face, bark something to the other attendant, and then speak angrily into her walkie-talkie. Next, Alla would say a few firm words. When she finished, the attendant would motion to her for us to come on. Alla would turn and motion to us. The angry man would put himself in our way and speak again, and the whole process would start over.

Though the misty rain and knifelike wind made the day seem colder than its 50 degrees, the 33 of us stood in our lightweight clothing without speaking or moving. We waited, and we prayed. We prayed that God would keep us from getting sick in spite of exposure to the harsh weather. We prayed that if God wanted us in Yalta, He'd get us there. He knew we had only two days to give out 28,000 Bibles. He knew we had no hotel reservations that night in Moscow.

We also prayed for the people standing beside us: the angry young man, the family with two small children, the grandmother and granddaughter, and all the rest. They had reasons too for wanting to make that Simferopol flight. They too were standing out in the chilling rain and wind.

We waited and prayed for what seemed like hours while the drama on the steps played itself out in front of us. Later, we learned the reason for the problem. Groups traveling on Aeroflot were required to arrive at the airport at least an hour before departure time. Because of unexpectedly heavy traffic, we had not arrived that early. While we were on the way, another flight to Simferopol had been canceled. The people who stood with us had been told they could get on our flight. Now, they were being told they couldn't, after all. They were arguing that we should have to wait because we hadn't shown up early enough.

Finally, breakthrough! A third uniformed woman arrived. She and the flight attendant with the walkie-talkie climbed the steps so that they could stand out of the rain to confer. The third woman apparently had more authority than the other two. At her nod, Alla gave us the nod, and we boarded. Those to the rear of our group literally had to push people out of their way in order to reach and climb the steps. As we entered the aircraft, soldiers arrived to "escort" the ones still standing at the foot of the plane back to the terminal.

Our wait that seemed like hours really lasted only 30 minutes. The people we left behind had waited a lifetime for breakthrough.

Drum Roll

You need a breakthrough. You realize it. In fact, you've grown desperate to see it happen. You've made the need a matter of fervent prayer. You've done everything you know to do to prepare the way.

The stage is set. The drum roll begins.

But no breakthrough happens. What do you do?

King David could have answered that. He experienced breakthrough quickly when he sought God's help against the Philistines. But just prior to the Philistines' attack, David enjoyed what was probably the major breakthrough of his life, though it came after years of delay. He was crowned king of Israel.

Israel's need for new leadership became apparent when David was still a boy. King Saul rejected God's commands one time too many. As a result, the Lord rejected Saul as king. God declared He would raise up a ruler who would follow Him with his whole heart; then He directed Samuel to anoint David to be that king.

At the time David was anointed, he was a shepherd. He continued to herd sheep until his one-boy victory over Goliath earned him a place in Saul's army.

Meanwhile, Saul was becoming not only more and more ungodly but also more and more deranged. Eventually jealousy drove him to try to kill his popular young commander. As a result, David spent years running for his life from Saul. During those years, David prayed often and fervently, expressing his heart cry for breakthrough. He obeyed God even to the point of refusing to take Saul's life twice when unexpected opportunity arose. Still, the obsessed king ruled.

Finally Saul and his heir, Jonathan, died in battle. Did Israel then rally to their hero and proclaim him king? No. Ten of the tribes declared Ish-bosheth, another of Saul's sons, their leader. Only the tribes of Judah and Benjamin followed David. Later, Ish-bosheth was murdered, though David had no part in the crime. In fact, he had the killers put to death. Subsequently, all Israel crowned David king.

Painfully, slowly, and by degrees, David experienced the break-through God had foretold. In the meantime, the king-to-be could only do one thing: wait.

The Rub

I admit it: waiting doesn't thrill me. I leave no slot for it in my jam-packed schedule. Even when I don't have a pressing appointment, I chafe to find myself following a slow motorist or halted by one of the lengthy freight trains that cross our road. Can you identify?

Beyond frustration, waiting often involves discomfort, or even pain. Because something you need, desire, or intend has not yet hap-pened, you must hold in check your sense of readiness or expectancy. As time passes, you tire from the effort required to keep that in-between pose while hope wars with disappointment. Once in a while, hope may gain a victory, which fresh disappointment quickly crushes. Hope then begins to seem not an ally but only a prelude to greater hurt, so you hold it at arm's length.

In the US today, millions of women wait to hear the news, "You're going to have a baby." Each month, they feel new pain when hope dies again. For years, my friend Beth and I were among the ones who wondered if we would ever experience that breakthrough.

Beth and her husband, Richard, and Jerry and I, were two of four couples who spent much time together. In early 1981 when Beth and Richard decided it was time to start a family, I was already struggling with the problem of childlessness.

Two-and-one-half years later, our friends Cindy and Don had their first baby girl. A year afterward, our other close friends, Katie and Gary, had their first son, Clint.

On the heels of Clint's birth, I learned great news: after seven years of marriage, Jerry and I were expecting a child. The killer was: I had to tell Beth.

Beth and Richard moved out of town in 1986, but still we four couples kept in close contact. Living in the Dallas-Fort Worth area with access to many top-notch physicians, the couple went through extensive testing, and Beth underwent two surgeries. On several occa-sions she was told, "The problem is corrected now. You should be pregnant within six months."

By early 1991, Cindy and Don had two girls and had just learned that a third child was on the way. Katie and Gary had two boys. Jerry and I had two girls. Beth and Richard still had no child.

Then, one evening in late March as I walked into the house after a church meeting, Jerry told me, "Beth wants you to call her." I knew before he finished the sentence what Beth wanted to tell me. After 14 years of marriage and 10 years of wanting a child, she and Richard were going to have a baby.

The Pain

Yes, waiting often hurts. But combine waiting with continued, often extreme, physical pain, and the magnitude of the hurt becomes almost unimaginable.

Mike Burczynski was my pastor for 5 years. Now in his mid-40s, Mike is one of the most godly men I know. He preaches powerfully; he prays powerfully. He prayed for breakthrough for Jerry and me the same month our first daughter was conceived.

But Mike is still waiting for breakthrough in one area of his own life. Since the age of 32, he has battled a kidney stone illness that has baffled specialists all over the country. In 1991 he told me his story.

"The first stone I ever had was 13 years ago in Pontotoc, Mississippi. I had gone to get some things in Tupelo for a pre-Christmas party my wife and I were giving for some pastor friends and their wives. I was checking out when I was doubled over with a terrific pain in my side. Thinking I must be dying, I left the shopping cart and went to my car.

"I was in the worst pain of my life for about an hour. Finally, I called a nurse who was a member of our church. She diagnosed the problem as a kidney stone and told me to go to the emergency room. I was X-rayed, seen by a radiologist, and passed that stone after two days in the hospital.

"I didn't have another kidney stone until about a year later. It took longer to pass—about a week. Then the stones began to come about every year for some time. I moved to Corinth, Mississippi. The stones came at about the same rate, but they took longer and longer to pass. At the end of my ministry there in 1987, I was having stones that would take up to a year to pass. By the time I moved to Idaho that same year, I had passed 28 kidney stones."

During the years Mike has suffered from kidney stones, he has also suffered frustration after frustration in seeking treatment. At first, he adhered to the typical treatment of changing his diet to limit the calcium and drinking lots of water. Though tests showed no deficiency that might cause the problem, he continued to have more stones.

Later, during what Mike thought was a kidney stone attack, a complete physical at a large city hospital showed no stone and no other reason for the severe pain. Yet, the pain persisted. Finally, a pathologist allowed Mike to diagnose himself. "Describe the pain you're feeling," he said. After Mike did, the pathologist asked, "What do you think is causing it?"

Mike said, "I still think it's a kidney stone."

The doctor responded, "Well, you ought to know by now." He then treated Mike by giving him an IV at high velocity. Two days later, Mike passed three stones.

On two other occasions, at two different medical facilities, X rays failed to show kidney stones that later passed. Finally, one specialist using a scope discovered the secret to the riddle: scar tissue had formed an obstruction in such a place that stones lodged there could not be seen by X ray.

But no specialist has solved the riddle of why the stones keep coming and why Mike's body continues to hold them for such extended times. As a result, Mike now lives in almost constant pain. He says, "The intensity of the pain varies greatly. On a scale of one to ten, with one being a mild headache and ten being close to passing out, I spend most of my time between three and six. There are times when the pain level is very low, but it is seldom that I don't have any pain whatsoever. I become unable to function very well at levels seven and eight. Beyond that pain threshold, I am generally forced to take something for pain and to lie down until the spasms subside. About a third of the time, I am in the disabling levels of pain."

Bittersweet

More than most of us, Mike Burczynski has experienced the pain of waiting for breakthrough. At this writing, he does not yet know how or when his wait will end. He says, "I have never gotten what I could call a crystal clear word from the Lord except the word Paul got from Christ in 2 Corinthians: 'My grace is sufficient for thee.'"

Mike says, "I still look for whatever means Christ might use to loose me from this pain." He adds, "I only hope that I endure with joy so that Christ might get whatever glory there is to be had in it all."

He uses the word *bittersweet* to describe the years of waiting for freedom from the kidney stones. Quoting the opening line of Dickens's *A Tale of Two Cities*, he quips, "It was the best of times, it was the worst of times."

Perhaps the tastes of bitterness and sweetness collided most explosively when Mike's illness brought him closest to death. In 1989 a secondary, and distinctly different, pain started. Doctors diagnosed the problem as Mekel's diverticulitis. Prescribed medicines, however, did not help. Less and less able to deal with "two points of pain," Mike talked with his doctor about surgery.

"It was to be a very simple surgery," Mike says. "They were sure that recovery should be rapid and the [secondary] problem solved."

When the surgery was performed, however, "the Mekel's was not found. A small irritated area of the bowel was resected, and my appendix was removed. All went well until the third day after surgery." That day, Mike began having what he calls "general discomfort." He tells what happened next:

"The fourth day, I knew something was drastically wrong. I realized intuitively that I was dying. My intestines were paralyzed; my temperature was rising higher and higher. I expected to die by the fifth day and was talking with Christ about what I thought would be my homegoing. I hurt for my wife, family, friends, and church because I knew it would cause them grief. I was, however, looking forward to being able to be close to Christ Jesus.

"Early in the morning, the Lord Jesus spoke to me clearly that He was not finished with me yet. Even though I did not appear any better, I had total assurance that I would recover.

"The recovery was ever-so-slow. The pain that had prompted the surgery was gone, even though it had been misdiagnosed. I had not drunk a drop of water or eaten a bit of food for nine days, and I had lost a good bit of weight, but it was good to know the Lord still had some work for me to do."

Bittersweet.

No one has to remind you that waiting can sometimes be a bitter experience. You might even describe it as "the worst of times." But have you also found it to be "the best of times"? Have you discovered and savored the sweet taste too?

Mike summarizes the sweetness he's experienced during his waiting times with two lines from a Gordon Jensen song: "Grace upon grace, like the waves on the shore, One on another they faithfully pour."

When waiting for breakthrough, you too can swallow the bitter and savor the sweet. How? Speaking as one still in waiting, Mike shares some insights.

Sit Tight

Mike Burczynski has his own amplified version of Isaiah 40:31a: "They that wait upon the Lord (like a servant waits before the throne ready to react to any royal command) shall renew their strength."

Mike's rendering of this familiar Scripture verse points out a truth: God honors waiting that is characterized by expectancy and trust, by firmness and constancy of mind. From God's viewpoint, those who *wait* are continually looking to and hoping in Him. You might say they have a "seated" mind-set.

Right there, most of us have problems. Do you? While waiting, do you do everything *but* sit tight mentally? Do you let your attention wander to everything *except* the One before Whom you stand? If so, you're no longer waiting, in the biblical sense. You're just passing time.

Don't Focus on the Situation

Sometimes your thoughts run to *the situation*. After fruitless hours spent trying to figure it out, you volley between discouragement and anger.

The last four years Jerry and I were childless, I believed I had a promise from the Lord that we *would* have children. That is, I believed it until I began looking too closely at the way things stood. Breakthrough seemed hopeless, and I would reinterpret God's promise in ways I thought He might be able to handle. Maybe He means I'll have "spiritual" children through my teaching and writing ministries?

With my eyes still on the situation, I avoided pregnant women, baby showers, and newborns. I cried through Mother's Day church services. One year, I expressed deep anger, both to God and to Jerry, for several months.

At my lowest point, God showed me Isaiah 50:10: "Who is among you that fears the Lord, That obeys the voice of His servant, That walks in darkness and has no light? Let him trust in the name of the Lord and rely on his God" (NASB). That Scripture verse hit me hard. It reminded me that before I could experience breakthrough in the area of childlessness, I had to learn how to wait.

Pondering the verse, I realized that in order to get to the other side of the darkness, I had to take my mind off appearances and focus again on God. Before knowing which way He would move, I had to trust Him to go the right way. I had to decide that, even if I had misunderstood His promise, it was OK; by His grace, I could be happy without children.

Once I chose to trust God, He enabled me to wait.

Don't Focus on Others' Remarks

Sometimes, we give our minds free reign to brood over *others' comments*. In 1990, in the weekly column I write for Corinth's local newspaper, I declared the Sunday after Mother's Day to be Women-Who-Aren't Mothers Day. Though my daughters were five and two at the time, I still hurt with those who wanted to be mothers, but weren't.

I wrote, "For 24 hours, no one will be allowed to look at a newborn and quip to the nearest woman-who-isn't-a-mother, 'When are *you* going to have one of those?' No one will give unwanted expert advice such as, 'Don't wait too long now. Your biological clock is ticking.' No one will treat a childless woman as if she's spending her life waiting for the other shoe to drop."

Of course, women-who-aren't-mothers aren't the only ones who have to deal with distressing comments. During Mike's years of kidney stone struggles, he's faced all kinds of remarks, mostly from well-meaning Christians. Bothered and bewildered at the seemingly endless attacks of pain he suffered, many tried to figure out both the reason and the cure.

"The judgmental types," says Mike, "wonder what kind of unrighteousness I am doing to have such a condition. The mad-at-God school see this as just one more example of the Lord's lack of compassion. The healer types have asked permission to pray for me in tongues, give me special oils to anoint with, send their pastors or healers to lay hands on me. (I have welcomed their concern and do not want to hinder the Lord if He chooses to heal by dramatic and miraculous means.) When they have given me their 'best shot,' they dismiss me as not having enough faith.

"There are those who are upset with me for not functioning sometimes, and I get the distinct feeling they consider me a loafer. There are those who simply treat it as though it does not exist. The 'Good Ship Lollipop' group tell me to put on a happy face and everything will be fine. Those of the stoic school say, 'Just use your willpower and set your mind to it and you can conquer the pain.'"

"Some are sympathetic and wish they could take my pain for a short time. Others say there must be a reason that will lead to greater spiritual power through the pain." If Mike were to let his mind run like a model train among all these perspectives, he'd soon feel not only dizzy but also defeated.

When you wait, beware of letting your thoughts go wherever others' remarks send you.

Don't Focus on Yourself

For Mike, the greatest threat to God-honoring waiting is self-pity. He says he often has pity parties to which he only invites three—me, myself, and I. If you've waited for something a long time, you may well have had such parties yourself. Self-pity is so natural that Mike doesn't advocate trying to correct it completely at one sitting. He believes our tendency to focus on self is recurrent and must be dealt with on a continuing basis.

As you wait, then, notice when you keep thinking about *me* and feeling sorry for *me*. And on each occasion, choose to turn your eyes outward again and to fix them on Jesus.

How to Sit

Once you've done all God requires to set the stage for breakthrough, He directs you to wait. He instructs you to sit tight mentally. He knows your mind tends to act like a preschooler turned loose in a toy store; but He never commands without enabling.

So how do you keep your renegade thoughts in check? How do you prevent your focus from being moved away from God? The answers Mike suggests are simple, yet demanding. They're simple because you've heard them before and can do them. They're demanding because to do them you will have to exercise discipline in the power of the Holy Spirit.

Note: Mike looks to both the Scriptures and prayer as the keys. He calls Bible reading "a great solace, as well as a goad to break up the pity party." He says, "Prayer is becoming more and more a constant state simply because I can't do without it while going through the hard times."

When in waiting, you may not feel like reading God's Word. Choose to read it anyway. If you don't, you will not be able to *wait* with hope, trust, and expectancy. When in waiting, you may want to spend your prayertime pleading for breakthrough or accusing God because He has not sent it. Do present your petitions to the Lord. Do be honest with Him about your feelings. But, know that petitions and accusations will not keep your mind focused expectantly on Him.

Do seek and claim God's promises. Yet realize that even the promises will not fully guard your mind. Rather, make knowing Him your priority. To help you know Him better, start a list of His attributes. Focus particularly on those divine qualities most needed in the situation you face. Repeat those qualities aloud. Tell God you're choosing to believe those truths about Him, regardless what your experience seems to say.

For example, you may read that He is the God of peace. At times you are most tempted to worry, call on Him as your peace. You may be able to quote, "God is light." When everything around you seems darkest, acknowledge Him as your Light.

Why Sit?

Why put all this effort into keeping your mind still before God? While waiting, why can't you wallow in whatever thoughts you want to think? There may be many reasons. Two come to mind.

First, those who wait with "seated" minds gain what all waiters long for: peace. Isaiah 26:3 declares, "You will keep in perfect peace him whose mind is steadfast, because he trusts in you" (NIV).

Second, while you wait with your thoughts fixed on Christ, an invisible bond grows between Him and you. The Hebrew word usually translated "wait" in the Old Testament can also mean "to bind together by twisting; to be joined."

Jerry and our two girls enjoy creating things with pipe cleaners. Often, they will take two wires of different colors and painstakingly twist them together to make what appears to be one wire with spiraling colors. They then use the new candy-cane looking sticks to make any number of other things. In cleaning up their concoctions, I've found that the wires they've twisted together from end to end are almost impossible to separate. From that day forward, the two are, for all practical purposes, one wire.

So it is when you wait for breakthrough with your mind poised Godward. His invisible hands intertwine your heart with His, creating a oneness that defies separation.

Stay Busy

Mike says biblical waiting is not only mentally focused, but also physically active. Vince, another committed minister (see chap. 3), echoes that truth. Vince says, "Waiting is not passive, but actively involved in pursuing obedience and adjusting to what God has for you today, yet all the while, expecting His answer to come at any time."

Donna, whose breakthrough experience is described in chapter 5, believes strongly in active waiting. She cautions against having a mind-set that says, every day, "I've got to have this breakthrough. I've got to have it." Such a mind-set can occur if we let *desperation* for breakthrough turn into *fixation* on breakthrough. *Desperation*, as described in chapter 2, is craving breakthrough badly enough that you're willing to do whatever God requires—including waiting. *Fixation* is impatience, trying to force God's hand.

Donna says, "I don't want to live my life just hoping that the time's going to pass for the next breakthrough because if I do that, I'm going to miss a lot of the real special joys God has for me in each and every day." To her, active waiting means living every day to the fullest. Believing God is working in her behalf all the while, she leaves her requests for breakthrough with Him and gives her time to:

- loving people,
- enjoying her family and her work,
- seeking balance in all areas of her life,
- seeing conflict not as a negative, but as a challenge,
- taking advantage of every opportunity to share Jesus with the people around her.

Donna wants even the waiting times to be times when she allows "the Lord in His special, special love to just shine through me."

How can you stay busy during waiting times? Here are some ideas.

1. Involve yourself in ministry.

If you've ever sat in a hospital room while someone you loved lay sick, you know how physically tiring waiting can be. The immobility combined with concern for the hurting one can so rob you of energy that getting up to do the smallest task becomes a major undertaking.

Any time you've felt the drain of waiting over an extended time, you may reach a point where doing anything, especially trying to help others, seems an impossibly big effort. You may just want to sit, but successful waiting means fighting the desire to go to sleep until it's all over. It means choosing not to let feelings of tiredness and frustration rule, but to keep on doing what God has called you to do, regardless.

While my friend Beth was waiting to have a child, she continued teaching elementary school. She could have chucked that ministry, feeling, "I just can't be around all these children when I can't have any of my own." Instead, she let God use her, year after year, as His witness in public schools.

When it comes to keeping on regardless, Mike puts most of us to shame. He says, "There are times when I must minister while in a great deal of pain and, of course, I dare not take any kind of pain medicine during those times. I sometimes have to witness, counsel, study, read, preach, lead, and many other pastoral duties when I would much prefer lying down. But, the Lord is very faithful and gives me bursts of grace-energy from time to time that are akin to the bread He gave Elijah which carried him for 40 days."

Make sure the ministries you're doing are those to which God has called you. Then, stay with them. Don't quit just because the going got rough. Along with Bible reading and prayer, ministry can refocus your thoughts on Christ. It can take you out of yourself and give you new perspective. Ministry done out of simple commitment to obey will also increase stamina. It will strengthen your bonding with the Lord.

2. Don't neglect R-and-R.

Two hobbies help Mike keep his mind off his pain and the problems associated with it: nature photography and falconry.

You may not choose the same activities, but do give part of your waiting time to creative rest and recreation. Beware of spending countless hours sitting in front of the TV. At the end of all those hours, you'll not feel refreshed, but only more lethargic and probably spiritually drained. Look for ways to include mental or physical activity in your leisure time.

If you find yourself chronically tired, check your sleep patterns. Seek God's grace in correcting what needs to be corrected. Have a physical checkup. Commit to a God-pleasing diet and exercise.

3. Treat limitations as boundaries, not prison bars.

While waiting for a husband to surrender to Christ, you may spend years going to church by yourself and missing many services you would like to attend.

While seeking a new job, you may go day after day to do work you consider confining or demeaning.

While waiting for breakthrough regarding physical weaknesses, the place you live, your children (or the lack of them), your marital status, or your commitment to aging parents, you may have to curb your own plans. In any waiting time, you may feel you're missing out on a major part of life.

Remember: every life has limitations. The boundaries differ from person to person. They will differ at various times in your own life. Wherever your limits are today, a holy God has set them. He intends them not to imprison you, but to guide and protect you. Your limitations become your prison only when you treat them as such.

Our oldest child, Megan, attends a school with a large playground surrounded by a fence. Outside the fence runs a major road down which vehicles travel at fairly high speeds. The fence, then, serves both as a boundary and a protection. Megan could spend her recess times standing at the fence crying because she can't go outside it—but she doesn't. She spends recess enjoying the freedom she has within the boundaries of the fence.

Ed Oliver worked for 32 years with greater limitations than he really wanted. All those years, Ed was involved in starting churches, and all those years, he lacked an effective tool for discipling believers. Then in 1982 Ed discovered MasterLife, a 26-week discipleship program. He says, "When I went through the five-day MasterLife workshop and saw the quality, the comprehensiveness, the attractiveness of the materials, and when I saw the methodology of the MasterLife 'process,' I felt the strong conviction, 'This is it! This is what I have needed throughout my ministry. From here on, I will make discipling the thrust of the remaining years of my active ministry, and I will use these materials in doing so.'"

For his remaining 8 years of full-time church work and now on a part-time basis in retirement, Ed has used the discipleship tool that was, for him, a breakthrough. Over those years, he's experienced great joy in leading small groups of believers and "seeing before my very eyes dramatic spiritual growth and fruitfulness."

But what of those earlier 32 years? During those years, he says, "I occupied the time by doing the best I could with the materials I had." Those may have seemed years of small victories. But God's Word asks, "Who despises the day of small things?" (Zech. 4:10a NIV). Certainly, our Lord does not. He who sets the boundaries delights when we make it our business to carry on within them.

Mike's kidney stones often curtail his activities. He says, "I simply try to take one day at a time and sometimes one hour at a time. I seek to do my pastoral duties in those times that I am physically able and rest when I can go no further. I feel sometimes like the Civil War soldier who wrote, 'Lay me down and bleed awhile and rise and fight again.'"

But what curtails Mike's ministry in some ways has enlarged it in other ways. He says, "I have been given some sweet revelations and sermon thoughts during the very time of intense pain." Similarly, David the shepherd-king penned some of his most beautiful psalms while "limited" by physical, mental, or spiritual suffering.

Mike adds, "I feel that the pain has humbled me. Also, I have a new empathy for those in pain that I would never have had apart from my own pain. I've been told by others, and felt myself, that I had an additional spiritual power in preaching during the duress of pain. I assume it is because of a total reliance upon Christ that is called for when we sense weakness. I can be better used to challenge people from the pulpit to sacrifice for Christ even when it hurts them to do so."

How do you handle your limitations? You can chafe under them, or grow frustrated and angry. You can give up in despair, or you can make the most of your life within its set limits. Only then will you find contentment and purpose and, in God's time and way, enlarged boundaries.

Turning Point

Some waiting times are short but intense, like the one our Yalta-bound team spent at the foot of an Aeroflot jet. Other waiting times stretch long and slow, like Mike's. The long-stretch type may take you way past the point where you think you will snap.

But no matter how many days, weeks, months, or years you may wait for a breakthrough, you can rest assured you haven't waited as long as Noah. He looked for a promised flood for nearly 100 years, and all that time, he really waited. Hebrews 11:7 says Noah had a mind-set of "holy fear" (NIV) during those decades. He kept busy that century building an ark to God's specifications and preaching to the ungodly people all around him.

Then one day, Noah walked with his family through the door of that ark, saw the door close, and heard rain on the roof. The waiting time was over. The breakthrough had come. Noah lived another three-and-one-half centuries afterward to enjoy the benefits of it.

I may wait long for something you receive quickly, or never even desire. But somewhere along the way, you too will wait for something. How do I know? Because God provides all His children training in waiting. He always custom designs His lessons.

We each experience different "waiting lessons." Yet, all who believe in Jesus Christ wait for the ultimate breakthrough. First Corinthians 15:51-52 describes it: "Listen to this secret truth: we shall not all die, but when the last trumpet sounds, we shall all be changed in an instant, as quickly as the blinking of an eye. For when the trumpet sounds, the dead will be raised, never to die again, and we shall all be changed" (TEV).

On that coming day, God will close up His lesson plan, walk to the door of heaven, and signal the trumpeter. In that moment, all waiting will end. We who know Christ will suddenly have new bodies that will never know wear and tear. We'll be changed! We'll live forever to enjoy the benefits of it.

"So then, my dear brothers [and sisters], stand firm and steady. Keep busy always in your work for the Lord, since you know that nothing you do in the Lord's service is ever useless" (1 Cor. 15:58 TEV).

Did you catch that? Sit tight. Stay busy. Know that nothing you do in the Lord's service is ever useless. Not even waiting.

5

BREAKTHROUGH!

"Whoever splits logs may be endangered by them"
(Eccl. 10:9 NIV).

On August 22, 1991, this fax was sent from Campus Crusade for Christ's Soviet Union director Dan Peterson in Moscow: "God has done an incredible miracle here in answer to prayer. To Him be all praise and glory and honor and power."

Wednesday, August 21

We awoke Wednesday morning to the reports that four people (actually only three) died overnight in street clashes and that the coup leaders, still in power, were amassing forces.

10:00 A.M., Moscow time

In response, 15 staff gathered in our apartment for a day of prayer and fasting. We watched the news on CNN at the top of the hour—then spent the rest of the hour in prayer. Our first hour was spent in praise, worship, and thanksgiving. The Lord gave us all great peace.

11:10 A.M.

Our next hour began with 15 minutes to confess any sin. We then began to give ourselves to intercession. We prayed for leaders, people, the situation, how God might use this takeover for His glory.

12:15 P.M.

I began our next season of prayer by asking the question, What do we really want to see God do? A whole nation hung in the balance—300 million people (souls). Did we only want safety and peace, or did we want to see God do something so mighty that the world might know that He was at work here? . . . We began (with little faith) to ask

God for this country, that somehow God would not allow repression
to triumph. . . . We asked Him to miraculously restore order and
democracy and thwart evil plans. We rebuked the devil's influence in
the name of Jesus.
3:30 P.M.

After a time of prayer we turned on the news. To our amazement
we learned that there were rumors that all coup leaders were trying to
flee the city. Later the report was confirmed. Within one more hour
we watched as tanks began to withdraw from the Kremlin and other
parts of the city. By 5:00 P.M. Russian TV was on the air broadcasting
the Russian parliament session. Boris Yeltsin was telling the people
what had taken place. By 7:00 P.M. it was announced that Gorbachev
was back in power and returning soon to Moscow.

What an incredible day! Our God reigns and hears the cries of
His people!

August 27
"Focus on the Family" mailout from James Dobson
"Dear Friend,

Today's date is August 27, 1991, which happens to be the 31st
anniversary of my marriage to a beautiful young lady named Shirley.
We are celebrating that occasion, so to speak, by spending 11 hours
aboard an American Airlines jet en route from London to Los
Angeles.

Many thoughts are tumbling through my mind as we streak across
the sky at 38,000 feet. Mostly, I wonder why the Lord took us to
London but chose not to permit us to continue on to Moscow as
planned. We suspected that the open doors in the Soviet Union might
soon close. That's why we elected to make this taxing journey just two
weeks before our move from Los Angeles to Colorado Springs. We felt
an urgency to share our respect for the institution of the family and
our love for Jesus Christ with the great Russian people. Thus, we spent
18 months planning this trip and thought we had every detail
arranged.

But there we sat in a London hotel, watching CNN and contem-
plating the possibility of civil war between Communist hard-liners and
the courageous democratic reformers. Our advisers in the State
Department, our friends in Russia, and even members of our board of
directors urged us to abort the trip. We complied, reluctantly. By the
time the coup had failed and peace was restored in Moscow, it was

impossible to reverse our decision. Besides, those who would have hosted us there had other things on their minds in the wake of the startling developments during that week. So here we are today on our way home, thinking about what might have been and hoping the trip can be rescheduled next spring.

What incredible events have unfolded in these past eight days!"

September 6

He told me his name was Muhamed. My next question was a natural: "Are you, then, of the Muslim faith?"

"My parents are Muslim," he said. "But I cannot embrace any faith that teaches polygamy. I am a victim of polygamy. My father had four wives."

I met Muhamed on the Moscow-to-Simferopol flight our Yalta-bound team almost didn't make. Boarding that jet after our 30-minute ordeal on the ground, I found a window seat with two empty seats beside it. An Enterpriser named Gayle sat beside me. Then the young man sat next to her.

I have no idea how that young man ended up in that seat—except that the Lord put him there. Members of our team were the last people to board the jumbo jet. Supposedly, everyone else who got on the plane was already seated.

But he was there. Gayle and I smiled in his direction, chatted briefly with each other, and then looked for something to do to occupy the two-and-one-half hour flight time. I pulled out my Bible. Gayle opened her travel journal and began to write.

"This might help," the young man said, indicating to Gayle the tray attached to the seat in front of her. We both looked at him in surprise. He spoke English!

That's when we found out his name was Muhamed. A doctor from Africa, he was studying obstetrics and gynecology at the Simferopol Medical Institute. He had a wife and baby in Simferopol.

I asked him, "Would you be interested in learning a bit about the Christian faith?"

"Yes," he answered.

While Gayle prayed, I explained Who Jesus was, why He had come to earth, how He had died and risen again, and what He offers all who entrust their lives to Him. Muhamed seemed especially moved when I told him Jesus could make him new from the inside. I said, "If you hold bitterness and an unforgiving attitude toward your father because of his polygamy, your heart is in chains. Jesus can set you free from those chains."

I explained how to receive Jesus as Lord. Then I asked, "Do you want to receive Christ now?" Muhamed said quietly, but firmly, "Yes."

"I don't want to rush you," I said. "Do you want to think about this further or to ask me any more questions?"

He paused just briefly. "No. I'm ready now."

So, in an aisle seat on a packed Aeroflot jumbo jet, 16 days after the breakthrough that allowed me to be there, Muhamed bowed his head and prayed aloud to receive Jesus Christ as his Lord and Saviour.

Breakthrough Brings Joy

Words can't express the joy I felt when Muhamed prayed to receive Christ. It made all the struggle to get to the Soviet Union, and to board that airplane, worthwhile. But, my joy in Muhamed's decision may well have been surpassed by the joy a woman named Judi felt when her friend Yuko made the same decision for Christ. Judi and her husband, Dennis, have served the Lord in Japan for more than ten years. They've found that decisions for Christ there rarely come quickly. Soon after arriving, Judi met Yuko. Yuko was not a Christian, yet she helped Judi begin a weekly Bible study. Over time, the two developed a deep friendship. Judi alerted many believers in the US to pray for Yuko.

Still, Yuko made no decision. It seemed that, just as she would make progress toward believing, something would result in her taking several steps backward. One Sunday morning after more than seven years of weekly Bible study, Yuko lingered when everyone else in the class left. She had a question about the lesson. "Do you mean that Jesus had a choice? He chose to die for me?"

Judi said, "Yes," and showed Yuko some supporting Scripture verses. Several times, Yuko repeated the question, and Judi repeated the answer. Then Yuko began to cry. Finally, the two prayed together, and Yuko invited Christ into her life. Judi experienced joy in Yuko's breakthrough—joy intensified by their close friendship and Judi's long wait.

Breakthroughs to salvation aren't the only ones that bring joy. Any breakthrough that reveals God's hand at work can elicit great rejoicing. Vince and his wife and children had become a one-car family. "We simply could not afford two cars," Vince says. Yet, he believed deeply that two cars were needed to provide his family transportation while he carried on his ministry among internationals in Seattle.

Further, Vince needed a vehicle that would hold family members *and* music instruments, including drums, guitar, and trumpet.

He and a few friends made the request a special prayer priority. Within six months, God had provided several thousand dollars from miscellaneous sources, as well as one $10,000 gift given simply because the person felt led to do so. Vince says the giver "had no idea that I was wrestling with God about a specific matter pertaining to transportation." When Vince was able to buy a used car with cash, he and his family rejoiced; the Lord of breakthrough showed His strength to provide.

If you've known breakthrough, you've known joy. And if you've known joy, you've expressed it. You may have shouted or whistled. You may have smiled or laughed. You may have jumped up and down. Or, like Deborah and Barak, you may have sung.

Deborah was a judge and prophetess in Israel. One day she called for Barak and gave him God's command: "Raise an army and attack the Canaanite troops that have cruelly oppressed Israel for 20 years. When you do, I am going to give breakthrough" (see Judg. 4:4-7).

Barak did as God said. He gathered 10,000 men from Israel's tribes and led them into battle. "On that day God subdued Jabin, the Canaanite king, before the Israelites. And the hand of the Israelites grew stronger and stronger against Jabin, the Canaanite king, until they destroyed him" (Judg. 4:23-24 NIV).

On that day too Deborah and Barak sang for joy: "When the princes in Israel take the lead, when the people willingly offer themselves—praise the Lord!" (Judg. 5:2 NIV).

Breakthrough Brings Repercussions

You've probably thrown a stone into a pond or lake. As the stone breaks through the surface of the water, it produces a ripple effect. Other types of breakthroughs also produce ripples. The fall of the Berlin Wall rippled all the way to Moscow and beyond. The failure of the Soviet coup rippled to an Aeroflot jet bound for Simferopol.

We enjoy the ripples a breakthrough yields, but we often don't expect or enjoy another kind of repercussion breakthrough produces. We might label it *backlash.*

Newton's third law of motion is that "to every action there is always an equal and opposite reaction." What is true in science is often true in life. As the writer of Ecclesiastes warns, "Whoever splits logs may be endangered by them" (Eccl. 10:9b NIV).

Backlash from People

When people see breakthrough from a twisted perspective, painful reactions may fly. Indeed, many biblical men and women faced such backlash.

•*Jacob* worked 14 years for his father-in-law, Laban, earning dowry money for his two wives (Laban's two daughters). Then Jacob decided to leave. He planned to establish his own sheep ranch back in Canaan.

Laban begged Jacob to stay. Finally, Jacob agreed, on the condition that Laban would give him all the spotted, speckled, and black sheep and goats as his wages. Jacob wanted those specific animals for a reason. "My honesty will testify for me in the future, whenever you check on the wages you have paid me. Any goat in my possession that is not speckled or spotted, or any lamb that is not dark-colored, will be considered stolen" (Gen. 30:33 NIV).

The two men agreed, and Jacob continued to raise Laban's flocks, while building his own. Genesis 30:43 declares, "In this way the man grew exceedingly prosperous" (NIV). (The Hebrew for "grew exceedingly prosperous" can also be translated "broke through.")

Soon Laban's sons were spreading the word, "Jacob has taken everything our father owned." Laban's own attitude toward Jacob "was not what it had been" (see Gen. 31:1-2). The backlash Jacob felt included jealousy and alienation.

•*Peter* was the disciple God used to break through to the Gentiles with the gospel. At God's insistent prompting, Peter went to the house of Cornelius, preached to the crowd of non-Jews gathered there, and saw the Holy Spirit fall on every person who heard the message. Peter and those with him were astonished. They decided the good news of salvation in Christ must be for *all* peoples.

However, not everyone understood or rejoiced in the breakthrough. In fact, circumcised believers in Jerusalem criticized Peter. Only when he "gave a complete account of what had happened from the very beginning" (see Acts 11:4) did the Jewish believers stop griping and start praising.

•*Gideon* defeated a vast army of Midianites with 300 men from the tribes of Manasseh, Asher, Zebulun, and Naphtali. The Ephraimites greeted the news with anger; Gideon hadn't asked their tribe to take part in the battle.

•*Mary* conceived Israel's Messiah while still a virgin. People assumed Jesus was illegitimate (see John 8:41).

•*Saul* of Tarsus made one of the most amazing turnarounds of all time. Instead of celebrating, fellow Jews immediately began trying to kill him.

While God-sent breakthroughs produce joy in those who see them for what they are, such breakthroughs can also produce everything from disinterest to anger, from misunderstanding to hatred in people who fail to see them correctly.

Backlash from Circumstances

Repercussions may also take the form of trials or problems. Such problems may follow naturally on the heels of sudden change, or they may not even seem related to the breakthrough. Either way, a wave of trials often hits the one who has met breakthrough just at the height of the joy.

Two issues of *Time* magazine illustrate how quickly this type of backlash can begin. The first of the two, dated September 2, 1991, was titled "The Russian Revolution." Thirty-seven of its pages focused on the breakthrough of a Communist coup turned inside out.

The very next issue, dated September 9, featured a cover photograph of Lenin splattered with blood. Titled "Power Vacuum," that issue devoted 21 pages to coverage of the backlash the Soviet people were already beginning to encounter: a disintegrating union, confusion over how many and what sorts of nations would replace it, political feuds, drastic economic woes, threat of a harsh winter and food shortages, and the potential rise of another repressive form of government.

About the same time, former Eastern bloc countries that officially buried communism many months earlier were experiencing backlash. In some areas, state churches threatened to replace atheistic religious repression with their own form of control. In at least one country, some people groups warred bitterly against one another. Communism merely changed names in many instances.

An article in *U.S. News & World Report* announced, "In Poland and across Eastern Europe, euphoria over the collapse of communism is giving way to squabbles over nationalism, economic austerity and ethnic identity. Democracy has no easy answers."[1]

Circumstantial backlash doesn't happen only on global levels; it happens to individuals too. Donna and her husband, Robert, began an awesome venture in 1988. They located in a rapidly growing area of Fengshan, Taiwan, and set out to start a church there. Knowing the difficulty of such a work, many people discouraged the couple from even trying. Others warned, "You cannot reach families here. You need to work with young people or singles, but you can't reach families."

Robert and Donna began with a Sunday morning worship service in their home. Many weeks during those first months only their family, a language teacher and her family, and one other language teacher attended. After the first year, the young church began to rent a building in what Donna describes as "an excellent location." By 1991 attendance at Sunday morning services averaged 30 to 40 people. Most of those coming regularly were family units, many with members who were doctors or other highly educated adults.

Instead of being discouraged by the relatively slow progress, Donna is thrilled. "It takes time for people to be able to be acquainted with the gospel," she explains. "It's not uncommon here at all to run into people who don't know Who Jesus is. They do not know anything about Christianity. And for me to expect them to make a decision to accept Christ when they don't even know Who He is, isn't very realistic in my opinion."

She and Robert see what has happened as breakthrough. "It's a miracle that we even have a church here," she says.

However, with the breakthrough came backlash. For one thing, the "impossible" job of starting a new church proved much more tiring than either had expected. The couple didn't have anyone working with them. Starting as they were from scratch, they felt they couldn't leave, even for vacations.

They threw themselves into the more than full-time task. At the same time, they struggled to fulfill family responsibilities. Their two older children, Lisa and Jonathan, attended boarding school a three-hour drive away. Nurturing the two meant making time for trips to visit them. Their youngest daughter, Lori, still lived at home and attended a school sponsored by the missionary group with whom the couple work. Donna and Robert were committed to spending time with Lori, as well as taking part in her school activities.

In addition, Robert was serving on the board of Lori's school. Donna was teaching English. She says, "My own priorities really got out of balance, trying to figure out how much time to give in the church planting situation while providing for my family's needs. I was trying to do *everything*. I really took on way too much and was very exhausted."

Besides the stress of an overly full schedule, Donna and Robert had to deal daily with the stress of living in a densely populated area with a culture so different from their own. Meanwhile, Donna came down with dengue fever. Hospitalized for about five days, she felt the effects of the fever for six to eight months. Those effects included total exhaustion and depression. Donna had never experienced depression before. She began reading whatever she could find to help her understand what was happening.

Then a string of crises hit. Their son Jonathan's roommate, Bryan, was killed in a canoeing accident. Their daughter Lori was hit by a motorcycle while crossing the road by the school. Donna's grandfather in the US, to whom she was very close, was killed in a car accident. Other family members back in the States became ill.

Almost simultaneously with breakthrough, flying splinters seemed to hit Donna and her family from a hundred different directions.

How to Handle the Joy

You're forewarned. Breakthroughs bring repercussions. You may be asking: How do I handle those repercussions? How do I deal with them so they don't completely negate the breakthroughs? You do need to know how to deal with the backlash. But first, you need to know how to deal with the joy.

Looking forward to breakthrough, you might not think handling the joy will be a problem. But think back to breakthroughs you've already experienced. In the excitement, did you or others do anything you now consider silly? Did you or they do anything you now consider harmful? The euphoria linked with breakthrough can sometimes be dangerous.

After Gideon's victory in battle, the elated Israelites made him a proposition: "Rule over us, both you and your son, also your son's son, for you have delivered us from the hand of Midian" (Judg. 8:22b NASB).

The people apparently didn't pray about the matter. They didn't ask God, "Do you want us to have a king? If so, is Gideon the man?" They didn't even think through the matter. They assumed that because Gideon had won one crucial battle, he would be a successful long-term leader. Yet great generals may make poor kings, and God's call to one task doesn't necessarily include the call to another.

In approaching Gideon, the Israelites also assumed that both his son and grandson would possess the outstanding leadership qualities he had displayed. They were willing to commit themselves to three generations of kings based on one victory. Their joy overran them.

Wisely, Gideon refused the people's offer; but then he let his own joy get in the way of wisdom. Calling for each Israelite to bring him one earring from the battle spoils, he used the gold to make a priestly garment called an ephod. Soon Gideon, his family, and all Israel were bowing before that ephod.

Like Gideon and the Israelites, we can make the mistake of letting the joy of breakthrough derail us—or we can keep our joy on track by keeping it turned Godward.

1. Turn joy to praise.

When breakthrough comes and you feel like singing or shouting or leaping, turn those expressions of joy toward the Lord and praise Him. Put your feelings into thoughts or words that give God the glory for what happened.

When others begin to pat you on the back for the part you played in a breakthrough, deflect that honor toward the Lord. If God wants you to offer your praise privately, say a sincere thank you to the one complimenting you. Then tell your Lord, "Father, So-and-so gave me this compliment, but I give it to You." When God leads you to speak your praise publicly, you might say, "Thank you so much for your kind words. God's strength (or faithfulness or love or grace, etc.) enabled me to do that."

If grand ideas come to you in the midst of your joy, lay those ideas at the feet of Jesus and leave them there while you praise Him. Then, if your ideas don't already sound foolish, ask Him for guidance in regard to them. Don't act until you know you're following His leading and not your own feelings.

Deborah and Barak handled their joy wisely after victory in battle. Instead of taking the credit for what God had done (as the Israelites tempted Gideon to do) or creating something that could become an idol (as Gideon did), they turned their joy to praise.

They sang their praises *to* the Lord. They sang the praises *of* the Lord. They sang in the hearing of the people. They rehearsed what had happened from God's standpoint. In so doing, Deborah and Barak kept things in perspective. They avoided making rash decisions while at the height of their joy. They avoided elevating themselves. They uplifted the Lord of breakthrough.

2. Turn joy to witness.

Sometimes when God works, you know He did it and other

Christians know He did it; but the unbelieving world knows only that a few believers are grinning like Cheshire cats.

When someone who doesn't know the Lord asks questions, you may be tempted to tell what happened, but not tell Who engineered it all. In so doing, you sidestep witnessing opportunities God has stationed in your path. By abusing the joy, you do both God and the one to whom you speak a disservice.

No encounter with any person is an accident. God orchestrates every "chance" meeting, every "chance" comment that might open the way for you to tell someone about Him. When you fail to turn joy to witness, you thwart heaven's plans, and you miss greater joy.

Vince rejoiced when he found a car that he was able to buy with cash; but he didn't just grin to himself about it. He used the opportunity to witness to the person who sold him the vehicle. Vince told his story of breakthrough and pointed the honor to God.

May you too handle your joy by turning it Godward.

How to Handle the Repercussions
You don't have to be crushed by whatever "equal and opposite reaction" follows the forceful action of breakthrough. Rather, you can deal victoriously with the backlash. The secret? Do with backlash the same thing you must do to deal successfully with the joy: expect it and direct it toward God.

As in other areas when you expect something jarring, brace yourself. Then, if splinters do fly, use your shield of faith to deflect those "fiery darts" toward Him Who can disarm them.

1. Brace yourself against accusations.

You've probably seen it happen: children are playing a game; one wins; the others start yelling, "You cheated!"

Something similar may happen to you. You experience a breakthrough. Instead of rejoicing with you, others begin pointing accusing fingers: "He played up to the boss." "She didn't deserve that honor."

You can't stop others from accusing, but you can make sure that any accusations leveled against you are unfounded. Jacob found that out. Regardless of what he did to show that his sheep and goats were not stolen, Laban's sons still spoke ill of him. Yet, whatever Laban's sons said, Jacob could point to the speckled, spotted, and black animals that made up his flocks. He had accumulated them honestly.

Another thing you can't do is to brace yourself against others' accusations in hit-or-miss fashion. You don't know where break-through will happen or how others will accuse. To be prepared, you have to focus day-by-day on godly living.

The Apostle Peter emphasized this point several times in his short first epistle. "Be holy in all that you do, just as God who called you is holy" (1 Peter 1:15 TEV), Peter said. "Your conduct among the hea-then should be so good that when they accuse you of being evildoers, they will have to recognize your good deeds and so praise God on the Day of his coming" (1 Peter 2:12 TEV).

Then, as if double underlining the point he'd already made, he wrote, "Keep your conscience clear, so that when you are insulted, those who speak evil of your good conduct as followers of Christ will become ashamed of what they say" (1 Peter 3:16 TEV).

You'll be ready for accusations if you're committed to behaving every day of your life in a manner pleasing to God. That doesn't mean you won't sin. It does mean you'll hurry to God with the sins you do commit and receive His forgiveness and cleansing for them. It also means you'll constantly seek to abandon sin and do right. You will never accept certain sins as ones you "just have to live with."

2. Brace yourself against others' wrong attitudes.

Just as you can't stop others from accusing you, you can't stop oth-ers from having wrong attitudes toward you. You can be prepared for any coolness, anger, or indifference that may come.

And again, you can't brace yourself in hit-or-miss fashion. The very ones you think will be most happy for you may be the ones who greet the news of your breakthrough with the most resentment.

To guard against people's unkind reactions, cultivate godly love. Peter also emphasized this point more than once. "Love one another earnestly with all your heart" (1 Peter 1:22b TEV), he urged. "Above everything, love one another earnestly" (1 Peter 4:8a TEV).

Paul lived out the principle of loving God's way, regardless. On the road to Damascus, he met Christ and experienced breakthrough. Soon afterward, the Jews of Damascus plotted to kill him. To save his life, several believers lowered Paul in a large basket at night through an opening in the city wall.

The rest of his life Paul faced hatred, anger, misunderstanding, and bitter resentment from his fellow Jews; but he didn't let their wrong attitudes undermine the breakthrough that had occurred. He didn't let their ungodly reactions breed ungodly reactions in him.

Rather, he chose to love them. He didn't feel good about the wrongs they did to him. Yet he kept spending himself on their behalf. At one point he said, "How great is my sorrow, how endless the pain in my heart for my people, my own flesh and blood! For their sake I could wish that I myself were under God's curse and separated from Christ" (Rom. 9:2-3 TEV).

If Christ Jesus lives in you, you can love with that kind of love too. Jesus is love. He chose to spend Himself on behalf of an angry, hostile world. He can do the same thing on a smaller scale through you.

His love, however, won't suddenly appear full-blown within you when others' bad attitudes surface. You cultivate His kind of love by consistently choosing to make loving choices toward others long before the breakthrough and backlash that may follow occur.

3. Brace yourself against discouragement.

Whether backlash arises from other people or from circumstances, it can jerk you down quickly. Elijah found that to be true. In rapid succession, he had experienced a series of breakthroughs: fire from heaven consumed a waterlogged sacrifice and altar; the wayward Israelites finally confessed, "The Lord alone is God!"; 450 prophets of Baal were slain; rain poured down after three-and-one-half years of drought.

Then pagan Queen Jezebel sent Elijah a message: "I'm going to kill you today." Suddenly, Elijah plunged from a new high to a new low—and it took him a while to recover.

But he did recover because long before Jezebel's threat, Elijah had a godly focus. He kept his eyes on God while standing before wicked King Ahab and predicting years of drought. He continued to look heavenward while living in hiding by the brook Cherith and eating food the ravens brought. He even kept looking to God when the brook dried up.

God did not disappoint him. The Lord sent Elijah to a widow who provided for him, her son, and herself from a bottomless bowl of flour and jar of oil. Thus, when backlash did send Elijah reeling, it only did so for a time. For a little while, he focused on the circumstances and on himself. But then, he turned his eyes back where they were accustomed to looking . . . to his God. (See 1 Kings 17.)

To brace yourself against discouragement, you too must develop a godly focus before backlash hits. First Peter 1:13b urges, "Set your hope completely on the blessing which will be given you when Jesus Christ is revealed" (TEV). If you place your confidence in anyone or anything closer at hand, disappointment may well knock you flat and hold you down.

But if you live expecting Jesus to win, you can take setbacks in stride. You may get discouraged momentarily, but you won't be defeated permanently.

4. Keep trusting.

To prepare for any repercussions breakthrough may bring, you've tried daily to choose godly living, godly love, and a godly focus. Then breakthrough occurs and one or more repercussions do follow. It's time to begin deflecting those repercussions toward God. But how do you do it?

When troubles and crises slapped Donna and her family like relentless waves, Donna rode them out by trusting in her God. While still hurting she kept believing, *God does use all circumstances in our lives to help us to grow and enrich us.*

She says her faith has been strengthened because of the repercussions. "But it's been strengthened in a kind of way where it's very realistic." Donna has learned that faith doesn't pray away every problem; it clings to God's grace in the midst of problems.

"We just hold on sometimes," she says. "We're very, very tired. But we hold on because we know that the Lord is going to be victorious."

If you too will hold on to the Lord when backlash hits, you'll find you're not the only one holding on. While you're clinging like a child to her father, and feeling perhaps that you're about to fall, "underneath are the everlasting arms" (Deut. 33:27 NASB).

5. Keep praying.

Don't ever stop praying about a major breakthrough when it happens. Instead, praise God for a while, and then begin to pray some more. Your requests will be somewhat different, but they should be just as intense.

Breakthrough occurred in the Soviet Union in 1990 when a law declaring religious freedom was signed. A year later, the breakthrough in the aftermath of the coup toppled the Communist system. As a result, one mission board issued what they called a "green alert" for the republics and states that had been the Soviet Union. "The upheaval in the Soviet Union has world significance beyond all capacity to describe," said the president of that board. He indicated the board would cut through many normal procedures in order to quickly deploy money and personnel needed to reach the peoples of the former Soviet republics with the gospel. "Unless we react immediately, we may not be able to take advantage of some of the opportunities."[2]

Announcement of the green alert came the day we stepped off the plane at Moscow, only two weeks after the coup, and before the fate of the USSR had been decided. Yet backlash in the religious arena had already started. For example, the heavily Muslim republic of Uzbekistan had, even then, voted to close its doors to missionaries. Cults such as Mormons and Jehovah's Witnesses were thrusting out missionaries into the area.

Lamont, our missions team leader, told us, "We have been given a window of opportunity and it sometimes seems to be a very limited opportunity. We'd better get with the program! These people's hearts are ripe! The Spirit is dealing with their hearts right now. The person who puts something in their hands now is the one who will reach them. We really don't have much time."[3]

Recognizing the importance of prayer in countering the backlash, the mission board trustees designated New Year's Eve 1991 as an international day of prayer for the new Commonwealth of Independent States, to kick off the green alert project. At the same time, other mission boards, missionary sending agencies, and evangelistic ministries were scurrying to take advantage of the Commonwealth's openness to the gospel. All were crying for believers to keep praying.

What's true in the international arena is also true in individual lives. If you want to see God complete what He has begun, you need to "pray at all times" (1 Thess. 5:17 TEV). Even after breakthrough.

6. Keep affirming the truth.

Gideon faced a crowd of angry Ephraimites. "Why didn't you call us when you went to fight Midian?" they yelled.

Peter faced a crowd of accusing Jews. "You fraternized with Gentiles," they said.

Both men met the backlash with wise words. Both spoke calmly to those taking issue with them. Both told the truth in a way that helped the unhappy ones see things from a different perspective.

Gideon said, "Look. All we did was blow trumpets, shatter pitchers, hold torches, and yell. When the Midianites started running, you joined in the battle and killed two of their best leaders. Your part was really the more important."

Peter began at the beginning and explained what God had done to get him to Cornelius's house. Then he told what God had done at Cornelius's house. When Peter's accusers heard this, "they stopped their criticism and praised God" (Acts 11:18a TEV). They couldn't argue with what so clearly bore the marks of God's hand.

When you face backlash, you too may be called on to speak the truth in love. You may have to do some explaining. You may need to do some perspective changing. Make sure you stick to the facts and express them in a positive, uplifting way. Make sure you keep your tone of voice calm and your manner firm but gentle. Others may come around, or they may not; but your words, if they are well chosen, will at least open the way.

7. Keep rejoicing.

Before I left for the Soviet Union, my orientation materials warned, "When you return, some people may show little interest or enthusiasm over what you have experienced. A few may accuse you of exaggerating or bragging. Do not let such people rob you of your joy."

Repercussions don't change the fact: you've experienced breakthrough. The Lord Who effected the breakthrough can also handle the repercussions. He is working all things together for good to those who love Him and are called according to His purpose. So, "Rejoice in the Lord always; again I will say, rejoice!" (Phil. 4:4 NASB).

Rejoice when the happy feelings engulf you. Rejoice when the ripples from breakthrough spread out farther than you'd ever imagined. Rejoice even when the repercussions hit. James Dobson didn't get to make his intended trip to Moscow in August 1991; but he still rejoiced in the breakthrough there.

Remember, "Whoever splits logs may be endangered by them." After reading this chapter, you know that when the axe breaks through the log, the splinters and wood chips may fly. You can prepare ahead of time for such eventualities. You can commit to dealing with the repercussions when they happen. And, like the experienced woodsman, you can still feel the joy when the sharpened blade falls and the impenetrable wood gives way.

6

WHEN BREAKTHROUGH HURTS

"He breaks through me with breach after breach"
(Job 16:14a NASB).

Donna, my roommate for our Soviet Union adventure, almost didn't make the trip. Her husband, Harold, and preschool daughters, Allison and Elena, drove her to Birmingham for orientation. When they left their mother, both daughters cried. Yet Donna enjoyed the get-acquainted time and opening prayer session on Saturday evening.

Then came Sunday morning, September 1. Donna and I ate breakfast in the motel restaurant. Afterward, we went up to our room to get ready for the morning session. We were sitting on our beds looking over the day's schedule when the phone rang.

Donna answered. "What are you doing calling this early?" she asked. A pause. Then she cried, "Oh, no! When?" Donna's 39-year-old brother, Elijah, had just died.

Donna knew Elijah was critically ill before she left home for Birmingham. She visited him in his hospital room, and he urged her not to change her plans on his account. He told her he was going to try to live until she returned and could show him her slides of the trip. But he said, "Even if I die while you're in Russia, don't come back early."

Elijah entrusted to Donna an English-language Bible and a letter addressed "To whoever receives this Bible." Elijah told Donna, "Give these to someone in the Soviet Union who can read English." Donna had hoped and prayed Elijah *would* live until her return. Now, grief and confusion flooded her.

Hanging up from her husband's call, she phoned her parents to find out what they wanted her to do. Elijah had died at 7:00 A.M. in his sleep. His mother, who was with him, told Donna, "About 6:30, Elijah was awake. The last thing he said before he drifted off to sleep was, 'Tell Donna good-bye for me. And tell her not to come back.'"

Donna's parents assured her, "He wanted you to go. And we want you to go." Donna prayed, and cried, and made her decision: she would go.

Early Monday morning, just before we left the motel for the airport, Donna got another call from Harold. Two-year-old Elena was sick. She was wheezing and vomiting. Previously, the same type symptoms meant pneumonia. Donna urged Harold to take Elena to the doctor first thing.

A little later, Donna called home again from the Birmingham airport. She learned Elena did have pneumonia, and the doctor had put her in the hospital. Still, Donna boarded the planes that took her on the first two legs of the flight.

In Philadelphia, she called home again. To her surprise, she found Elena had improved dramatically and had already been released. Still grieving over her brother and concerned over her child, Donna traveled with the rest of us to Moscow and did remarkably well for most of the week.

Then, crisis hit. While standing in the cold rain on Friday afternoon, waiting to learn if we would make the Moscow to Simferopol flight, Donna got a sore throat. The illness, added to the stress she already carried, overwhelmed her. She cried, off and on, our whole first evening in Yalta and all the next day.

Somehow, she hid her feelings from almost everyone until Saturday night. Then, when six Enterprisers met for a devotional time, Donna confessed, "I need prayer." Of course, she was experiencing grief. Even more, she said, she was struggling with guilt over leaving her family during their mourning time.

Five of us gathered around Donna and prayed for her. We prayed in Jesus' name that Satan would be bound and Donna would be freed to grieve, but to grieve without guilt.

Breakthrough Against You

Donna was trying to obey God's call. She and Harold believe the Lord wants them to spend their lives sharing the good news of Jesus Christ somewhere among the states of the former Soviet Union. Preparing to do just that, they were attending a Bible college in Florida. Donna was also working to help make ends meet. Both felt the opportunity for her to join the Enterprisers team was God-sent.

The Lord provided the money for the trip. He enabled the couple to work out provisions for childcare. The sacrifices the two made seemed small next to the joy of anticipation they felt.

Time came for the trip. Donna said good-bye to her brother and daughters, trusting God to take care of them. Then, just at the point of her obedience, it seemed God broke through against her. Instead of holding back illness and death, He loosed them.

Donna's experience isn't unique. The Bible abounds with examples of breakthroughs that caused grief. You can probably name someone who is right now reeling from a breakthrough that brought sorrow instead of joy. Somewhere along the way, *you've* probably felt that God broke through, not *for* you, but *against* you.

When breakthrough hurts, you may cry out. You may ask, "Why?" "How long?" "What do I do?"

Why?

Heavy rains swept through the city of Chihuahua, Mexico, the night of September 22, 1990. Raging waters overflowed dams, overturned cars, destroyed houses, and killed people. The force of the flood shattered a six-foot-high block fence. It broke through the back of one home, knocked down the walls, and swept away everything inside. In another house, the current tore a two-year-old child from his grandmother's grasp and carried him away. Immediately after the disaster, 45 people were known dead, 200 were missing, and 5,000 families had suffered loss.

Why? Why did such a devastating breakthrough happen? In Old Testament times, the psalmist Asaph expressed the same question. Couching his heart cry in poetic terms, he described the nation Israel as a choice vine. God had carefully dug up this vine from Egypt. He replanted the vine in Canaan. He nurtured and protected it so that "its roots went deep, and it spread out over the whole land" (Psalm 80:9*b* TEV).

But then God apparently broke through against the nation He Himself had planted. Asaph cried, "Why?"

"Why did you break down the fences around it? Now anyone passing by can steal its grapes; wild hogs trample it down, and wild animals feed on it. Our enemies have set it on fire and cut it down" (Psalm 80:12-13,16*a* TEV).

When breakthrough devastates, you too may be quick to ask why. Why is a good question if, in asking it, you become a seeker, and not an accuser. Accusers use why to point a finger at God. They ask, but do not expect or listen for an answer. Seekers use why to probe life's *contraries*, the things that don't seem to fit. Seekers accept God's silences, yet are willing to listen, even when the answer is one they'd rather not hear.

To Confront Deliberate Sin

God often levies painful breakthroughs to crumble walls of sin. Such walls are not built in a day. They go up brick by brick, as one person or many keep choosing their own way and ignoring God's.

Jehoram became king of Judah when he was 32 years old. His father, Jehoshaphat, served 25 years as a godly king, but Jehoram didn't follow his dad's example. When he became king, he had all his brothers murdered so they would pose no threat to his throne. He married into the family of wicked King Ahab and began to implement in Judah the wickedness Ahab had brought about in Israel. Turning his back on the Lord God, he led his people in idol worship.

As a result, God broke through against Jehoram. He allowed Edom and Libnah, two nations that had been under Judah's thumb, to revolt. He aroused hostile Philistines and Arabs against Jehoram; they invaded Judah and carried off all Jehoram's possessions, wives, and sons. God then allowed Jehoram to contract a lingering and incurable disease of the intestines. After two years of suffering, Jehoram died in agony, ending his eight-year rule over Judah.

The sister nations of Israel and Judah built their own sin walls. Like Jehoram, they chose time and again to do what they wanted, regardless of what God said. Through His prophets, God warned the Israelites that if they didn't dismantle the wall, He would break through it.

Israel persisted until she fell to Assyrian invaders. Soon Judah also tottered on the brink of disaster. Still Judah's remaining leaders continued not only to build their sin wall, but also to whitewash it. They insisted, "Everything's all right. No repentance is necessary. We're God's people. He's going to protect us."

God, however, had a different idea. He announced through the prophet Ezekiel, "In my anger I will send a strong wind, pouring rain, and hailstones to destroy the wall. I intend to break down the wall they whitewashed, to shatter it, and to leave the foundation stones bare. It will collapse and kill you all. Then everyone will know that I am the Lord" (Ezek. 13:13-14 TEV). And God was as good as His word.

Has the Lord ever broken through against you because you deliberately bypassed repentance? Are you, even now, erecting walls God will have to break through in order to get your life back on track? Have you ever tried to whitewash a sin you wouldn't relinquish? Are you trying to justify or to hide anything God calls wrong?

No matter what today's TV shows or movies may tell you, God hasn't lowered His standards. He still hates lying and stealing, whatever form they may take. He still opposes pride, greed, uncontrolled anger, and defiance of authority. He has never laughed or winked at sexual immorality. He is ever repulsed by those who call themselves His people yet who worship something or someone other than Him.

You may build a wall high and long. You may convince yourself that such walls are acceptable now; but one day, breakthrough will come. The wall will shatter, and it will fall on you.

To Expose Careless Sin
David usually obeyed God and longed to please Him. But one day, by his carelessness, David set the stage for God to break through against him.

The whole thing started innocently enough. King David decided to bring the ark of God to Jerusalem. The ark symbolized God's presence with Israel since the wilderness years. Once in Canaan, the ark rested at Shiloh until the days of Samuel.

Then God allowed enemy Philistines to take the ark in battle. At the time, Eli's daughter-in-law cried, "The glory has departed from Israel, for the ark of God was taken" (1 Sam. 4:22 NASB).

The Philistines couldn't handle the ark. Everywhere they took it plagues, confusion, and death followed. Finally, the Philistines loaded the ark onto a new cart pulled by two cows and sent it back to Israel. The ark came to rest in the town of Kiriath Jearim, and there it stayed for 20 years. During that time, Saul became king, reigned, and died. Later, David took the throne. Soon afterward, he decided to go get the ark so God's glory would dwell again in the midst of His people. David had commendable desire.

But he did the right thing in the wrong way. Instead of searching God's law to find out how to transport the ark, David copied the Philistines. Instead of calling for the Levites to carry the ark on poles made just for that purpose, David called for a new cart. On the way to Jerusalem, the oxen nearly upset their precious cargo. A man named Uzzah reached out to steady it. Immediately, he fell down dead.

Second Samuel 6:8 says, "And David became angry because the Lord broke through a breakthrough against Uzzah" (author's paraphrase). David named the spot Perez-Uzzah, the Breakthrough of Uzzah.

Later, after his anger had cooled, David came to understand the reason for God's action. Moreover, David corrected his carelessness. Planning a second, and successful, attempt to get the ark to Jerusalem, he told the temple helpers, "It was because you, the Levites, did not bring it up the first time that the Lord our God broke out in anger against us. We did not inquire of him about how to do it in the prescribed way" (1 Chron. 15:13 NIV).

Have you ever felt you were doing right, only to have God apparently break through against you? In such cases, did you double-check to make sure you *were* doing the right thing and doing it the right way?

You may be wondering how to make such a double check, or how to know "the right way" in the first place. Like David, you can find God's way in God's Word. The Bible gives His eternal truths. The Holy Spirit, living within every Christian, can teach you how His truths apply to any given situation. For direction, you can go to the Scriptures with a question or decision and search until His Spirit makes clear to you that you have found the answer. You can confirm that answer by waiting for God to bring circumstances in line with the direction He's given and by seeking out godly counselors.

All this takes time and effort, and you may chafe to be moving ahead. You may feel such effort just isn't necessary. You may assume that because a path seems right, it is right. Perhaps you may assume that because you understand *what* God wants you to do, you know *how* He wants you to do it. *Assuming* is not a synonym for *seeking*. It is an act of carelessness that almost always leads to trouble.

Fair Warning

Sometimes, as with David, God lets us follow our carelessness to its own result. Then He allows a painful breakthrough to correct us. Other times, the Lord warns us before we commit a careless act.

The young nation of Israel left Egypt and arrived at the foot of Mount Sinai. The Lord told Moses, "Consecrate the people today and tomorrow. On the third day, I will come down on the mountain in a thick cloud in the sight of everyone." (See Ex. 19:10-11.)

When God came down, Moses was to go up to meet Him, but no one else was to go near God. In fact, the Lord ordered boundaries to be set up all the way around the mountain. He warned the people not even to touch the foot of the mountain, on penalty of death.

Moses relayed God's orders to the people. Together, the Israelites observed the two days of consecration. Then, the third day, Moses brought all the people out to the foot of the mountain. After God descended on the mountain in an awesome display of power, Moses went up to meet God.

God greeted Moses with these words: "Go down, warn the people, lest they break through to the Lord to gaze, and many of them perish" (Ex. 19:21 NASB).

Moses had told the people exactly what God had said. He'd set up the boundaries around the mountain. He'd climbed all the way to the top. He said, "But Lord, we've already warned the people."

God told Moses, "Go back down, warn them again, and then come back up." Then God explained the reason for repeating the warning: "If they break through to come up to Me, I will break through against them." So Moses went back down the mountain and stressed God's warning one more time before climbing again into God's presence. (See Ex. 19:24.)

Are you listening closely for God's warnings? Might He be trying to speak to you about an area where you've previously obeyed, but lately grown lax? If so, heed Him and avoid pain you don't need to suffer.

To Build Up

I recently watched a demolition crew dismantle an old brick building in a matter of hours. Within a week, a new structure appeared in its place. Why was the old building removed? It no longer served any purpose. It was empty. The company that had used it moved to another location.

The new building housed a quick-stop grocery and gas station. It soon opened for business; but the new business could not have appeared without breakthrough. If someone hadn't been willing to shatter the old, no one could have built up the new. Sometimes God will send breakthrough in your life for the same reason. He wants to tear down what is empty, useless, even potentially harmful, so He can build up what He knows will be useful and good.

According to Ecclesiastes 3:3b, God sets "the time for tearing down and the time for building" (TEV). You may sometimes question

His timetable. While understanding the need for the tearing down, you wonder why it has to happen *now*.

Other times you may question God's selection. What He sees as empty and useless may look innocent or even "good" to you. In such cases, He may be trying to rid you, not of sin, but of clutter, and you may tend to cling to clutter. Or, you see things going to shambles that you count valuable, such as a marriage or a ministry, a person's life or a church body.

God counts those things valuable too. He values people so highly He sacrificed His Son for us, but He is willing to do shattering works in lives and relationships in order to rebuild them better and stronger.

Sometimes those shattering works go far beyond what you think you need or can take. Speaking of the God he had worshiped faithfully, Job cried, "I was at ease, but He shattered me, And He has grasped me by the neck and shaken me to pieces; . . . He breaks through me with breach after breach" (Job 16:12,14b NASB).

Job didn't know it, but God was doing a good work in his life, preparing to deepen him spiritually. Emerging from his suffering, Job declared the difference between the way he knew God before breakthrough and after: "In the past I knew only what others had told me, but now I have seen you with my own eyes" (Job 42:5 TEV).

Breakthrough to Pain

Loretta grew up in a dysfunctional family. "My parents were both hurting to such an extent that it was difficult for them to function in healthy ways as parents," she explains. Retta's dad was an alcoholic; neither parent was active in church. An only child, Retta experienced a great deal of trauma during her childhood and as a result sustained severe emotional damage.

In order to cope, she buried the painful parts of her life, blocking out whole years from her memory. She lived in what she calls "a survivor mode," focusing all her energies on achieving whatever lay at hand to achieve.

From the time Retta was a toddler, her grandmother took her to church. During her teenage years, Retta stayed active in church life. At age 15, she announced to the congregation that she was "surrendering for special service." She thought that meant she would be a missionary nurse. But once she got to college, the strenuous nurse's training caused her to begin to recall her childhood trauma. Unable to continue, she switched her major to elementary education.

She says, "With that decision, my call to missions, I thought, was dead." But several years later, God led Retta and her pastor-husband, Tim, into a mission setting in the United States. While serving in a struggling church in upstate New York, the couple began to sense God's call even farther afield. However, they had trouble nailing down that call.

"For a process of about eight years, off and on, we would contact a mission board. They would send us the preliminary information sheets, and we would fill those out and send them back. Then they would send the next part of the application process to us, and we would discontinue. We did that three or four times. We thought we must surely hold the world's record for how many of those little yellow sheets we had filled out and not returned."

Finally Retta, who had the most reservations, turned everything over to God. She says, "We went through all that paperwork, went through the appointment process lickety-split, were appointed and packed and crated and off to orientation and on the field, hardly before we knew what had happened."

"The field" for Retta and Tim was Korea. Moving from a small town in the South, where Tim pastored after New York, they settled in Seoul, a city of some 10 million. The couple and their daughter Lori lived in a high-rise apartment. Tim and Retta spent two full years in language school.

Retta explained that they had to commute downtown on subways so crowded that they couldn't have fallen down if they had wanted to. Then, for four hours, they would undergo the stress of language classes.

"In the East, the teacher is very much of an authority, almost a revered authority," Retta explains. "There is one way to do anything. The student must never argue with the teacher. Learning takes place by recitation and by lecture. The class is geared to either the teacher's pace or the pace of the brightest student."

After school and commuting home, the exhausted couple would still face two to three hours of homework. Then Lori would arrive home from school, "and there was parenting to be done. Against that background, the original trauma that I had sustained as a child began to resurface," says Retta. "Situations in adapting to a new culture, as it were, punched my button subconsciously and began to bring out anxiety and depression that I couldn't account for.

"I was pleased to be in Korea. It was where I wanted to be. I was where I knew that God wanted me to be. Yet the many stressors began to build. The more the stress began to build, the harder I worked and the faster I ran from all that cumulative pain. The pain that was never experienced and validated and expressed as a child began to spill over and get all mixed up with the stress and the pain and the difficulty of adjusting to a foreign culture. Of course I didn't know all that at the time. I just knew I was working very hard, and the tougher things got, the tougher I worked."

Retta and Tim finished language school and moved "down country" to begin their ministry. For two more years, Retta continued to ignore the warning signals. She pushed herself to do the work. In November 1988, however, Retta went to a missionary doctor in Pusan. She told him, "I'm just not able to function anymore. If someone doesn't do something soon, I'm either going to end my life or else get on a train or bus and just disappear."

The doctor and his wife took Retta into their home for two weeks while Tim got the house closed up and the family's things packed to go to the States on furlough. Dr. Jim later told Retta that she showed all eight major symptoms of depression while in his home.

She says, "One night in particular, I just totally broke. I was lying in bed crying, wailing like a wild animal. Barbara held me in her arms. Jim was nearby. She sang to me, as you would to a child. And it was just Jesus and me and all that pain.

"When I woke up the next morning, I was totally broken. I had broken through to pain. I thought the mission board would hate me forever, and have nothing more to do with me. I thought I would never be able to function as a wife and mother again. I thought I would never be able to take care of my family . . . never be able to take care of me again.

"I looked awful. I could barely walk from the bed to the bathroom. The only reality I knew was pain. I was afraid to live, and I was afraid to die. And all that pain I had run from all my life I felt in those first moments after the breakdown."

Retta and her family returned to the States. The mission board not only did not disown her, but lovingly supported her and her family. She started working with a therapist at a well-known Christian clinic. He wanted her to be admitted to the clinic; she wanted to undergo therapy on an outpatient basis.

She says, "It was just before Christmas. And I didn't want to be institutionalized because of the stigma, not just for me, but for our daughter. So we moved into a house God provided for us ten minutes away from the clinic. And I tried the very best I could to begin to heal. But I just couldn't. I couldn't function. I couldn't face life. Try as I would, I just could not cook a meal or help my daughter with her homework. And again I began to feel suicidal."

When Retta admitted her state to her therapist, he strongly urged her to be admitted to the hospital. As a result, she spent a month of inpatient therapy. She says, "When I think of that experience, although it was a private hospital with a dedicated staff of Christian therapists and lovely surroundings, all I can describe it as is 'breakthrough to pain.' Pain. Isolation. Loneliness. Hurt. Desperation.

"There were no longer any ways to defend against the hurt. There was no work to do, no role to play. All my roles were taken away. All the things I had always worked for and thought important were taken away. All that was there was me and that pain and a trained staff to make me face that pain."

After Retta was released from the hospital, she worked with a therapist on an outpatient basis. During the following months, she continued to improve physically and emotionally. When time came for the family to go back to Korea, she was functioning well. Her therapist wrote a letter to the mission board saying, "No guarantees, but she deserves a chance to try." At this writing, Retta is still serving with her husband in Korea.

She says, "The breakthrough to pain led me to a second breakthrough—and that is the breakthrough to humanity. I didn't know I could express pain, or any other human emotion, because it had seemed to me growing up that my pain caused a great deal of burden and inconvenience to the people I depended on. Since I didn't know where to take my need, I buried it. I didn't feel or experience it. Once I broke through to pain, I could not contain my pain. It was too great. Then I had to learn that it's OK to need others, to hurt, to need comfort, to cry, to ask someone to hold us while we cry."

Retta says, "As I have experienced the joy and the strength and the freedom of being me, with all of my emotions, pleasant ones and unpleasant ones, I have become alive."

How Long?

In my laundry room, I have a clothes dryer that can be set two ways. I can turn the knob to a timer. If I do, the dryer will quit after a certain number of minutes, regardless of the state of the clothes inside. I can turn the knob another direction to operate a heat-sensor switch.

Then, when the clothes get to a certain degree of dryness, the machine will stop. I rarely use the timer. No matter how many minutes it takes, I want my clothes to stop drying when they're "just right."

When you're feeling the heat of a painful breakthrough, you may ask, "How long?" You may want God to give His answer in minutes or days; but God doesn't usually deal with His children on those terms. He has other means for determining when the breakthrough has done its work.

Forever

After an old clothes factory in my town burned, it stood as a community eyesore for some time. Then, workers began to dismantle it. When enough of the building had been removed, the roof collapsed. For some reason, the workers left the task soon afterward. As of this writing, the rubble still lies where the building stood.

Psalm 28 describes those God will break down and not rebuild: "They take no notice of what the Lord has done or of what he has made" (Psalm 28:5b TEV). What has God done? He has sent His Son to pay the penalty for sin with His own blood. Many don't care. God has raised Jesus Christ from the dead. Many aren't impressed. What has God made? He's made a way for anyone who will to pass from death into life—few take notice.

One day, those who refuse to acknowledge and accept what Jesus has done for them will face the shattering breakthrough of God's final judgment. With all they've accumulated in this life reduced to rubble, they will agonize in eternal ruin.

You're skeptical? You don't believe a loving God would do such a thing? The God of patience and mercy is also just. His true Word contains graphic warnings: He will eventually break through against all who reject Him, and their pain will last forever.

Till One Zealous for God Intervenes

Phinehas prayed with a spear.

The Israelites who camped just outside the Promised Land became friendly with the Moabites on whose land they camped. Too friendly. Soon, the Israelites were involved in pagan worship. God's anger broke through against them in the form of a plague. Twenty-four thousand people died, and no end was in sight.

While everyone else mourned, one man paraded right through the middle of camp with his pagan mistress. A priest named Phinehas followed the two into their tent and plunged a spear through them both. The result? "The plague was stopped."

In this gruesome story the Bible identifies Phinehas as an intercessor, one who "stood up and intervened" (Psalm 106:30 NIV). The word translated "intervened" in that verse can mean "prayed." And according to the following verse, Phinehas's spear prayer "was credited to him as righteousness for endless generations to come" (NIV). God took no pleasure in letting a plague devastate His people, but His righteousness demanded that He do it. Phinehas's drastic measures satisfied God's righteous anger and so freed Him to show His mercy.

God takes no pleasure in causing anyone grief or pain. In fact, He searches out people who are willing to take drastic measures to stay His hand of judgment. He seeks intercessors. He is not asking you to kill other people. Rather, He wants you to mount spiritual attacks against the sin that destroys lives and invites devastating breakthrough. He urges you to step boldly in front of those to whom He in His righteousness must deal blow after blow.

Jesus Himself set the example, taking drastic measures against sin, not by wielding the spear, but by yielding Himself. His intervention spared all who believe in Him from the final fatal breakthrough when God will judge all people. If not for Christ, every person who has ever lived would be condemned to eternal death by his or her own sin.

One mother, greatly burdened over her rebellious son, intervened to stop God's breakthrough against him. After checking into a motel where she could be alone, she fasted and prayed for three days. At the end of that time, she believed she had God's promise that her son would return to the Lord. Her adult son is now a committed Christian.

The book *Rees Howells, Intercessor* by Norman Grubb, tells the life story of a man known for his ministry of intercession. A Welshman, Rees Howells served the Lord through the first half of the twentieth century. He believed in taking drastic measures to "gain the position" of intercessor. To stand in the gap for others effectively, Howells went to great lengths to (1) die to self and (2) identify with the one in whose behalf he pleaded.

On one occasion, when praying for a woman dying of consumption, he told God he would be willing to have the disease and even to die with it in her place. Another time, when praying for a dying man, Howells committed himself to take care of the man's wife and children should the man die.

The sick woman died, but the man recovered. At that point, Howells believed he had gained the position of intercessor for the sick by his willingness to identify with them in their suffering and even to lay down his life for them. From that point on, Howells intervened before God to bring healing to many, many lives.

Till God Completes What He's About

More than ten times, psalmists asked the Lord, "How long?" Apparently God was silent. No psalm records an answer to the question. Jeremiah, Habakkuk, and other prophets cried, "How long, O Lord?" To none of them did God give an ending date.

In Revelation the Christian martyrs ask, "Almighty Lord, holy and true! How long will it be until you judge the people on earth and punish them for killing us?" (Rev. 6:10 TEV). To them, God gives His most direct biblical answer to the how long question, and it isn't as specific as we might like. The martyrs "were told to rest a little while longer, until the complete number of their fellow servants and brothers were killed, as they had been" (Rev. 6:11b TEV).

How long? A little while. How long? Until God's purpose is accomplished. A strange purpose for a loving, almighty God: to complete the number of martyrs. If you were in charge, you would probably purpose to stop the killing of believers immediately and forever; but you aren't in charge. You aren't God; and He *is* loving and almighty, and beyond earthly knowledge.

Some of His purposes seem harsh. Jeremiah asked, "O you sword of the Lord, how long will it be before you are quiet?" Then Jeremiah answered his own question: "How can it [the sword of the Lord] be quiet when the Lord has given it an assignment to discharge?" (Jer. 47:7a AMP).

God sometimes wields a sword. Yet, He does not fling it around wildly, at random. Every parry, every thrust has a purpose. Each is served with perfect precision. In dealing with His own children, God's ultimate goal is never to maim or kill, but rather to separate and cleanse. Whether He's attacking sin, cutting away hindrances to further growth, or doing another work within us, He has our good in mind.

When His loving purpose is complete, He calls a halt to the pain. As Jeremiah said, "Though he brings grief, he will show compassion, so great is his unfailing love" (Lam. 3:32 NIV).

No Storybook Ending

Connie, in her mid-30s, has experienced grief and God's unfailing love as a result of breakthrough in her own life. While spending an evening at home with her husband and three daughters, the telephone rang. A stranger's voice on the other end of the line said, "Hello, Connie. This is your mother."

Shortly afterward, Connie flew to another state to meet a woman she hadn't seen since she was 3 years old. The meeting was wonderful. Connie found that she and Jewel, her mom, look almost identical, except for the age difference. "The moment I touched her, I knew she was my mother," Connie says.

Jewel and Connie talked a long time that day, and have been in contact since. Connie loves her mother. She's glad they found each other. But she says, "It's not a storybook tale. It's not, 'My long-lost mother found me, and we all lived happily ever after.'"

The reunion brought back much old pain for Connie; it introduced new pain. Through talking with Jewel, Connie has put together what appears to be the truth about her earliest past; but Connie says, "Many of the pieces are still missing."

Connie was born to a poor, young, waitress-mother and an affluent, vicious father. Connie says, "My mother was wild. She'll admit it." Connie's dad was worse than wild. "Mother said he tried to kill us. He locked her and all three of us children in the house one time with the gas on. He put cigarette butts out on her. He beat her." She adds, "He was capable of anything; I know that from experience."

When Jewel divorced Connie's father on the grounds of cruel, inhumane treatment, she got custody of Connie and her two older brothers. Later, when Connie was only 3, Jewel left her children with an aunt while she went to Texas to remarry. While she was away, Connie's paternal grandmother, Nell, took Connie from her aunt's. Jewel returned, went to Nell's house, and picked up her daughter while she was playing in the yard.

Nell had Jewel arrested for kidnapping. Connie says, "Mother told me the last time she saw me, my grandmother was ripping me out of her arms through a police car window." While Jewel was in jail, Nell and her husband, Alec, apparently set in motion two plans to make sure Jewel didn't get Connie back.

"They bought off the judge," says Connie. "He gave my grandmother custody of me on the grounds that Mother had abandoned me." At the same time, Nell created a new birth certificate for

Connie. On the new certificate, Connie's name, place of birth, and date of birth were changed—and Nell and Alec were named as her parents.

Connie's mother was released and effectively run out of town. Nell and Alec began telling Connie they were her mother and daddy. They said her uncle and her father, both of whom also lived with them, were her brothers. Connie lived in the same room with her natural father. She says, "From as early as I can remember, he abused me—physically, mentally, emotionally, sexually. Although everyone in the family was sworn to secrecy, he told me he was my father and that he could do anything he wanted with me."

When Alec and Nell learned that Connie knew who her real father was, they fell back on their second line of defense. They told her, "Yes, you're adopted. Your mother abandoned you, and that's why we have you."

The two apparently did not know about the abuse. Connie's natural father told Connie not to tell anyone. He threatened her with dire consequences if she did, and Connie never told. Not until she was an adult did she speak to anyone about what her father had done to her. Why? She feared her father. She didn't think her adopted mother, Nell, would believe her. She didn't want confrontation. She wanted only to shove the hurt to the back, to let it die. Above all, she didn't want to hurt Alec, her adopted father.

Alec was the bright spot in Connie's childhood. "He loved me better than anything," she says. "He thought I hung the moon. He was the only reason I grew up sane. He's the only reason I know how to love."

Connie thinks Alec helped Nell kidnap her because he had convinced himself it was best for her. Afterward, he was blinded to much that went on in the household. She says, "Growing up with him as my daddy was worth everything else I went through."

When Connie was 12, her natural father left. She's never seen him again. The worst of the hurt left with him, but the churning inside her stayed. It "never, ever went away," she recalls. "I didn't know how to be calm about anything."

Without really understanding why, she felt she had somehow missed her childhood. An uncle later told her that, as a small girl, she seemed like an adult in a little child's body.

Yet, Connie grew into womanhood with a gentle spirit, a sense of humor, and a deep appreciation for life. The churning stopped when, as a wife of two years whose marriage was already troubled, she went to her mother-in-law for counseling. The mother-in-law, a strong Christian, led Connie to a personal faith in the Lord Jesus.

Connie's marriage immediately made a turnaround. Eventually three girls were born to the couple. As a mother herself, Connie began to want to get in touch with her own mother. She asked different family members to help her, but no one ever gave her any useful information. She had given up the search when her mother called.

In the wake of that call and the visit that followed, Connie re-lived much she had tried to bury. She learned of wrongs she didn't even know she'd suffered. Jewel gave Connie her real birth certificate. Connie had to adjust to a new name, a new birthplace, and a new birthday, in addition to a new parent.

Since that first meeting with her mother, Connie has faced other new hurts. She has struggled with the feeling that neither her mother nor her adopted mother have told her the whole truth. She is also struggling to understand a new wrinkle: Jewel and Nell have suddenly become big buddies. Connie says their relationship reeks of ulterior motives, rather than the righting of old wrongs. She feels the two are trying to drag her into a situation where deceit plays a major part.

She has no idea what God's purpose is in allowing a breakthrough which continues to bring her pain. She doesn't know how long the pain will last. But she firmly believes God will do in this situation what He has done with all the other hurts of her life: He will turn everything horrible around to good.

Reflecting on all the bad that happened to her as a child, Connie says, "There was a purpose: everything worked out the way God want-ed it to work out and even better than I could have hoped it would." She believes this pain too will end when a loving God knows it has accomplished its intended purpose.

What Do I Do?
What do you do about unwanted breakthroughs? How do you handle them?

Avoid Unnecessary Hurt
Some painful breakthroughs don't have to happen. You can avoid them by taking two vital steps.

1. Make sure you belong to Christ.

The Lord Jesus loves you so much He laid down His life for you. He died on a Roman cross to pay the penalty for every wrong you have ever done or will do. He intervened between you and eternal death.

His intervention is not complete, however, until you've accepted it. Imagine a train on a track that has been washed away several miles ahead. The train is headed for disaster. Between the train and the disaster lies an intersection where the cars can veer off onto another track; but to make that vital adjustment, someone must realize the danger. Someone must pull the switch that will send the train onto the other track.

Jesus Christ has made a way for you to miss disaster. He laid Himself down as "the Way" to life. However, you won't just automatically end up on His track. You have to recognize that the way you're headed without Him is lethal. You have to pull the switch. You have to surrender your life to His Lordship.

Have you done that at some point in your life? If not, will you make that decision now?

2. Stay close to Christ.

Hosea 13:4-9 describes a deadly pattern you might easily follow. God has delivered you out of slavery to sin. You've acknowledged Him as Lord and Saviour. He's providing for you. You're delighting in walking with Him, enjoying the intimacy of His presence; but somewhere along the way, you begin to distance yourself from Him.
   •You become satisfied.
   •You become proud.
   •You forget God.
   •You set yourself against God.

Then God breaks through against you. "Like a bear robbed of her cubs, I will attack them and rip them open. Like a lion I will devour them" (Hos. 13:8 NIV).

You can avoid such breakthroughs by choosing not to take the first step in the wrong direction. Wandering away from God is easy, unless you set your heart and mind on *not* wandering away. If you keep alert and seek to stay close to your Lord, He will warn you when satisfaction or any other subtly wrong attitude tries to creep in.

Even if you do start down a path that moves you away from Him, you don't have to follow it to the bitter end. By His grace, you can realize you've stepped away. You can turn and run back to Christ.

Take a minute to lay your life beside the pattern above. Where do you fit in? Are you walking with God? Are you feeling the effects of a painful breakthrough brought on by your own sin? Or are you somewhere in between? Are your feet even one step away from the Master's?

Avoid the hurt you don't have to experience. Pray whatever prayer of confession or commitment will move you and keep you intimately joined to the Lord Jesus. You must make the choice. Your steps will go where your will directs them.

Go Through Needed Hurt

Lottie Moon, a missionary to China for 39 years, once said, "I do not believe that any trouble comes upon us unless it is needed."[1] At the time, Miss Moon and her family were trying to survive the Civil War. The war eventually stripped them of almost all their possessions, including Viewmont, the family estate.

Miss Moon didn't live in denial of what was happening, nor did she try to run from it. Rather, she clung to the Lord and lived through it. The lessons she learned from the war and its aftermath stood her in good stead during the nearly four decades she lived and ministered in China. She weathered many storms there because she set her face to go through them.

If you run or refuse when God is trying to do a breakthrough work in your life, He may bide His time for a while, and then start it all over again.

If you're reeling from a blow to your life or ministry, ask your Lord to show you whether any willful or careless sin has, even in part, brought on the blow. Ask Him to point out any area in which you assumed, rather than sought, His will. Ask Him to reveal anything to which you're clinging that you need to release. Be quick to hear and act on whatever He says.

If He shows you nothing that needs correcting, choose to believe that His workings, no matter how harsh they may seem, are good. Let Him minister to you the peace that is better than understanding.

Then, regardless of the reason for the pain, determine not to try to back out of the hurt or to go around it, but to move *through* it as quickly as He will allow. Choose, by God's grace, not to end up back where you started, or off in left field somewhere, but to finish victoriously on the other side of the pain.

After Retta suffered a breakdown overseas, she could have stopped the healing process anywhere along the way—but she didn't.

She chose to cooperate with Christian therapists, even when the therapy seemed to her "sheer hell." She spent months learning to let go of destructive behavior patterns and replace them with new, healthy ones.

After she and her family returned to Korea, she began experiencing flashbacks. A sight or sound would trigger a memory buried in her subconscious. As a result, she relived several times of being left alone or abused, times so traumatic she had previously blocked them out completely.

After each flashback, she spent three or four days in bed, her mind and body in shock. Of her husband, Tim, she says, "When the flashbacks would come, he was right there with me. He sat by my bed. I called him 'my human paraclete.' If it hadn't been for him, I wouldn't have made it."

Retta's therapist back in the States encouraged her long distance. "You're getting well. And it's OK."

Retta has realized that she could not fully trust herself to God or others until she got to the other side of agonizing breakthrough. She says, "The personal triumph of breakthrough is indeed worth the pain. Tough as it is, the triumph and the health and the freedom and the life I have experienced and the growth I've made are enough motivation to make me keep trying."

Retta believes, "Breakthrough is health. Breakthrough is energy. Breakthrough is life and worth the struggle. Oh, people, it is worth the struggle."

7

WHEN BREAKTHROUGH
DOESN'T COME

"My strength has perished,
And so has my hope from the Lord"
(Lam. 3:18 NASB).

In Yalta

About dusk on Friday, we were at the Simferopol airport boarding the bus that would take us to Yalta. We'd had a full day, and we still had to face the two-hour ride over the mountains. As we settled in for the trip our Yalta team leader, Alfred, made two announcements. The dinner we were supposed to have that night with Crimean pastors had been canceled due to our late arrival; the 28,000 Bibles we had planned to hand out in Yalta were still in boxes in Simferopol. Because Simferopol was much more centrally located in the Crimea, the supervising pastor who met us at the airport insisted on leaving the Bibles there, to be distributed later to area pastors.

We had planned to leave most of the Bibles with the pastors anyway. We knew they and their church members could take the Testaments into places we could never reach in a three-day visit to the area; but we had wanted to present the Bibles ourselves to the pastors when we gathered with them in Yalta. We had come around the world for the purpose of placing a number of those Bibles personally in the hands of people living or vacationing in Yalta.

After reaching the Hotel Oreanda, where we were to stay, we trooped into the hotel restaurant for a late supper. To our surprise, we found the restaurant was also the lounge. Unable to hear each other over the Russian rock music, we sat watching as tourists in evening dress drank and danced.

God used that situation to show us something. The tourists visiting Yalta were among the few Soviet citizens who had money to travel, to stay in hotels, to eat in restaurants, and to patronize lounges. Most of them were probably Communist party members; and just a few days earlier, Gorbachev had shattered the Communist party in the Soviet Union. What an opportunity to present God's truth to many who had just had the rug pulled out from under them! But how could we do it without Testaments in their language?

After dinner, the Enterprisers on the Yalta team strolled down the city's seaside promenade with flashlights in hand. We found an unlighted pier that stretched into the Black Sea. On that pier, we gathered to have our evening devotional. As a chilling breeze swept the sea beneath us, the water churned and broke against the pier.

We sang, "There's a call comes ringing o'er the restless waves, 'Send the light! Send the light!'"[1] We prayed, "Father, in Jesus' name, please loose any of those New Testaments You want us to hand out."

The next morning, 6,000 of the Russian New Testaments arrived in Yalta. That day and the next, we distributed the Bibles in six different locations in and around the city. Everywhere we stopped, as happened in Moscow, people flocked to receive the Testaments.

Meanwhile in Bishkek

Enterprisers leader, Andrea Mullins, recorded the experiences of the team members who separated from us on Friday in Moscow.

"The excitement of our taking Bibles to Bishkek in Kirghizia began to heighten as we boarded Aeroflot in Moscow on Friday morning. We gave away every Bible we had in Moscow because we knew 28,000 more were waiting for us in Bishkek.

"All the smells of the Soviet Union greeted us as we entered the plane. Inside, the same disrepair we observed in Moscow provided us with seat belts that didn't work, seats that fell back into the lap of the person behind us, and a toilet that only the desperate would use!

"As we made the 2,000 mile, seven-hour trip to Kirghizia, we gave Russian language tracts and other materials that proclaimed the gospel we had come to share to persons on the plane. Hunger for the gospel was evident. Everyone to whom we gave a tract would sit and read it over and over. As they left the plane, they would thank us again and again.

"We finally arrived in Kirghizia, a republic on the border of China. It was hard to comprehend that we had entered an area where few American Christians have ever been. As we looked out the windows of our bus, we saw a flat, dry, dusty city; but rising up behind it were mountains so high we mistook them for clouds. In the daylight the next day, we discovered a mountain range of treacherous-looking peaks, covered with snow, rising as high as 19,000 feet. The vision was so spectacular we were overcome with awe.

"Bishkek proved to be a city of great scientific advancement, a place where scholars from around the world come to study such things as seismology. Yet it also caused us to feel as though we had stepped back in time, with peasants walking their cows across a field.

"It wasn't long before we experienced the Muslim culture of the Kirghiz people. As we entered our hotel and tried to go to our rooms, the Kirghiz staying in the hotel made aggressive and threatening actions toward our team. Though we were conservatively dressed by Western standards, every young woman team member was propositioned.

"God protected us, and we learned very quickly that our stay in Bishkek would be very different from our stay in Moscow. The European Russians' attitude was far removed from the Kirghiz Muslim attitude.

"The morning after our arrival we went to breakfast, excited to find out how we would be distributing the New Testaments in Bishkek. But instead of Bibles, we were greeted with the news that the Bibles had not come and would not arrive in time for our distribution project because they were not yet printed.

"The team was visibly upset. Wasn't this our reason for coming so far? Our churches and others had invested so much in us so we could bring the Bible to people who did not have one. How could we witness without Bibles to give? We did not speak the language. We didn't have enough tracts to do much of anything! There was great frustration, even anger in the group, as each team member tried to sort out how such a thing could happen after all our planning. Probably to this day, if we took a vote within our team, they would still desire to have had the Bibles to give away in Bishkek."

When Hope Ends
Sometimes, you reach the end of hope. The breakthrough you've longed for, prayed for, prepared for, and waited for hasn't come—and, from all evidence, it won't. What then?

You may feel discouraged, angry, or bitter. You may withdraw; you may lash out at God or others. You may find it hard to stop crying or, weighed down with grief, you may find yourself unable to cry.

Whatever your feelings, don't try to hide them or to pretend they're not there. Don't let them consume you either. Take them to God. Lay them before Him. Be honest with Him about them. Jeremiah said, "Pour out your heart like water before the presence of the Lord" (Lam. 2:19b NASB).

Then, when you've emptied yourself before God, take a new look at the situation. Ask Him to show you what has caused you to give up hope.

Crisis Point

Sometimes, perhaps without realizing it, you may pin your hopes for breakthrough to a specific time or event. You just know that if ever it's going to happen, it's going to happen now. You've built a strong expectancy; now you're ready for the breakthrough.

What you are not ready for is the crisis point to pass without breakthrough. And when it does, your hopes are crushed. Yet, if you'll step back and look again, you will realize breakthrough can still occur. The chances of its happening may seem even more remote than before. The waiting time will be prolonged. Yet, what you've experienced is not the death of all hope, but the death of immediate hope.

A childless woman longing for a baby passes just such a crisis point each month. Her body gives evidence that she is still not pregnant. Once again, her breakthrough has not happened. She sinks a little lower into despair.

A person addicted to alcohol or drugs goes through a rehabilitation program and seems to be making a fresh start. Family members hold their breath. Is the breakthrough happening? Then, without warning, the one who seemed free repeats the addictive pattern. The family grieves.

Finale

"It isn't over till it's over."

It's a good saying—it points to the fact that sometimes we give up too soon. However, there are times when a point arrives beyond which breakthrough is no longer possible. Sometimes it's over.

Missions team members who traveled to Bishkek knew no breakthrough was possible when they learned the New Testaments they'd traveled thousands of miles to distribute had not even been printed yet; but the pain they experienced was small compared to what Craig's family felt at the moment of their finale.

Craig wasn't quite 30 when he went to the doctor with severely infected sinuses. His wife, Nancy, was expecting their first child. After weeks of medical guessing and testing, Craig underwent surgery to remove a mass behind one eye. Still, doctors had trouble pinpointing his problem. The mass was primarily infection, but appeared to contain a few cancer cells. Finally, a second group of doctors confirmed the diagnosis: Craig had lymphoma.

He began chemotherapy, but complications kept interfering. The chemotherapy caused Craig's white blood count to drop dramatically, and the lowered white count reduced his body's ability to fight the remaining infection. Later, cancer cells were found in his eye. By then, apparently, the cancer was in his bloodstream.

Craig lay very ill in the hospital on the day Nancy gave birth to their son, Alan Michael. His family wheeled him across the street to the Women's Clinic for the delivery, then back to his own room. A week later, Craig improved tremendously and was released. However, just before Alan turned three months old, Craig returned to the hospital, sank quickly into critical condition, and died.

Hundreds of Christians had joined family members in praying for Craig's healing. We know that when Craig died, he experienced the ultimate healing all believers enjoy on entering God's presence; but he didn't experience the breakthrough we had pleaded for.

As in Craig's case, death is often the point at which all hope for a certain breakthrough ends. Thank God, Craig was a committed Christian. His death caused great grief, but no spiritual regrets. Sometimes, though, a loved one refuses to turn to Christ, or to return to Him. When the last breath is taken, the possibility for turnaround dies.

That's Ricky's story. Ricky died of pneumonia. At least, that's what the family told—and pneumonia *was* what finally killed him.

Ricky died of AIDS. That's what people whispered, or said aloud when the family wasn't around. They weren't just spreading rumors; they were telling the truth. Ricky's untimely death can be traced beyond both pneumonia and AIDS, however.

Ricky grew up in church and made a profession of faith early. Bubbly and always smiling, he was a favorite with everyone. But somewhere along the way, he took a wrong step, and then another, and another.

At last, caught up in a homosexual lifestyle, Ricky dropped out of church. He grew more and more confused about right and wrong, about God, about his relationship to Christ. Believers talked to him, wept in prayer for him, and later wept over the news that he had suffered alone in a city far from home and, finally, died. The epitaph No Breakthrough had to be written across his life.

Death isn't the only point past which breakthrough is no longer possible. You may face other situations that have The End written all over them.

Jeremiah did. He wrote the book of Lamentations to describe the end of a whole nation's hope. Jeremiah had watched the kingdom of Judah descend further and further into godlessness. He prayed and pleaded for revival. "Wash the evil from your heart, so that you may be saved" (Jer. 4:14 TEV), he cried.

For 40 years the prophet sought breakthrough; but in 586 B.C. Judah's capital city fell to Babylonian troops and was destroyed. Jeremiah vividly describes the results: "How lonely lies Jerusalem, once so full of people! All night long she cries; tears run down her cheeks. Her people live in other lands, with no place to call their own, surrounded by enemies, with no way to escape. The city gates stand empty, and Zion is in agony" (Lam. 1:1-4, author's paraphrase).

He who had warned and warned now wept and wept. "My strength has perished," he cried. "And so has my hope from the Lord" (Lam. 3:18 NASB).

Forewarning

Sometimes hope leaves with a word from the Lord. At those times, God warns in advance that breakthrough will not come. He may speak through natural means, such as a doctor's report, or He may speak through a sermon or Scripture passage. However He chooses to communicate, you know in your spirit that you have heard from God. You may not like what you've heard; you may try to deny what you've heard; but deep inside you know He has spoken.

Jeremiah experienced this death to hope. Twenty years before Jerusalem's final fall to Babylon, God told him, "Jeremiah, do not pray for these people. Do not cry or pray on their behalf; do not plead with me, for I will not listen to you" (Jer. 7:16 TEV).

The Lord commanded Jeremiah to continue speaking His truth to the people, yet He warned, "You will call them, but they will not answer" (Jer. 7:27b TEV). What an assignment! Do all you can to bring about breakthrough; but it won't come. The situation's hopeless. The people for and with whom you plead have gone too far too long.

More than 2,000 years later, God forewarned the Apostle Paul not to expect breakthrough in an area where he longed to see it. Paul had a "thorn in the flesh" that he begged the Lord to remove. The third time Paul prayed about the matter God told him, in effect, "I will not send breakthrough. Rather, I will give you grace to live without it." (See 2 Cor. 12:8.)

Toward Hope Again

When breakthrough doesn't come, you have a choice. You can run *from* God, or you can run *to* Him.

At times when you lose hope, you may initially turn in anger away from the Lord. By continuing in that direction, however, you will only plunge yourself deeper into despair. At such times, against all odds, choose hope. By God's grace, make two impossible moves:

(1) Halt your spiral into hopelessness long enough to allow the Lord to show you whether crisis, forewarning, or finale has occurred.

(2) Climb toward hope again by choosing to turn to God. Express your faith in Him by taking three steps the prophet Jeremiah took.

Remember His Great Love

Jeremiah hit bottom. Though he had predicted Jerusalem's fall for years, the event shattered him. As he wrote Lamentations, he recorded the horrors around him, the darkness within. "My hope is gone," he cried.

Then, suddenly, his tone changed: "Yet this I call to mind and therefore I have hope: Because of the Lord's great love we are not consumed, for his compassions never fail. They are new every morning; great is your faithfulness" (Lam. 3:21-23 NIV).

In his lowest moment, Jeremiah turned to the Lord. He deliberately focused his thoughts on God. In fact, he rehearsed three of the Lord's attributes that seemed most to be missing.

"Because of the Lord's great love," Jeremiah testified, "we are not consumed." The Hebrew word translated "great love" is *chesed*. A key Old Testament word, it is so full of meaning that translators have trouble finding a synonym in English. Besides "great love," the New International Version renders it "mercy," "love," "unfailing kindness," "unfailing love," and "wonderful love." New American Standard almost always translates it "loving-kindness."

Chesed, a covenant word, carries the idea of loyalty, strength, and generosity, as well as kindness. It pictures the unfathomable quality that caused God to offer His only Son to die in our place.

God's "compassions never fail," declared Jeremiah. The word *compassions* comes from the Hebrew word for "womb." By using the intense plural form of the word, Jeremiah indicates that God cares for His people as tenderly as a mother cares for the unborn child she feels moving within her.

"Great is your faithfulness," Jeremiah cried. One who is faithful is steady, firm, and worthy of trust, with stability that stabilizes others. When circumstances seemed to shout, "God? No loving, compassionate, faithful God exists!" Jeremiah recalled, "Yes, He does."

In the years before Jerusalem's fall, Jeremiah saw God openly display His deep, loyal love. Now, Jeremiah caught only a glimpse of God's love in His choosing not to completely annihilate the people of Judah. Yet, even when the prophet could barely see the Lord's faithfulness and compassion, he chose to believe they were there.

When you face shattering situations, reflect on ways God has shown His trustworthiness and His tender concern to you in the past. Memorize and begin to quote Lamentations 3:21-23. Focus your mind on God's great love.

"God Is Here"

Carol is a pastoral counselor to AIDS victims and their families. Until recently, she worked at Cook County Hospital in Chicago. Her ministry there brought her into daily contact with suffering and death.

Some deaths were especially hard for Carol to handle. One young man who had contracted AIDS through homosexual relations had a conservative Christian background. He felt a great sense of guilt about his gay lifestyle, but would not lay that guilt at Jesus' feet, forgive himself, or allow others to forgive him. He pushed away anyone who tried to help, including hospital personnel and his own family. According to Carol, he died angry, alone, and alienated.

Two others who had been IV drug users had quite different stories. After discovering they had AIDS, they were able, for the first time in their lives, to get their lives together. Carol says, "They got off drugs, reconnected with their families, and were doing quite well on a personal and spiritual level; and then they died." She grieved for them.

When Carol began work at the hospital, a friend urged her to say over and over to herself, "God is here." She tried it, but at first the words came out as a question, "God is here?" Then she began to realize that God *was* there, expressing His love through people. In fact, He had called her to that place in order to demonstrate His love through her to the suffering ones.

She says, "The incarnation didn't just happen once. It happens every day. We're created in God's image for the purpose of loving and helping others. If we live our lives as closely as we can to our godly understanding of it, we help to bring God's presence into the lives of other people."

The sentence Carol still repeated to herself became a statement: "God is here." But sometimes the suffering just seemed too intense—and on those occasions, Carol's faith in God's love might slip. Then, she says, the AIDS patients themselves would "often remind me that there is a God of love. Many of them sense God's presence with them in the midst of the suffering. When I ceased to believe, they believed."

At that point, Carol's statement became an exclamation. Moving among the poor, the unwashed, the homeless, and the dying, she could exclaim, "God is here!"

When you lose hope, remember that God is not the unloving, powerless, or absent God circumstances may indicate. Voice your faith in Him, even if that faith is timid and halting. Like Jeremiah, keep believing and declaring "God is love." Like Carol, keep believing and declaring "God is here," even when you see no evidence.

Wait for His Compassion

You're driving along a mountain highway on a cloudless day. You round a curve and see this sign: Turn on Headlights, Tunnel Ahead. Two minutes later, you enter the tunnel.

The sun was shining before you entered the darkness. The sun will still be shining when you exit it. In fact, the sun is shining the whole time you're in the darkness: you just can't see it.

When breakthrough doesn't happen, you enter a tunnel. While passing through it, recall the sunshine of God's love you enjoyed before entering the darkness. Remember that God's sun is still shining, though for the life of you, you cannot now feel its effects. Realize that one day you will move out of the tunnel into the full glow of the sunlight again.

Jeremiah said, "The Lord is good to those whose hope is in him, to the one who seeks him; it is good to wait quietly for the salvation of the Lord. For men are not cast off by the Lord forever. Though He

brings grief, he will show compassion, so great is his unfailing love"
(Lam. 3:25-26, 31-32 NIV).

"Lord, Where Is Your Mercy?"
Angelique served as the national women's leader of her denomination.
Her husband had a good dental practice. Life seemed to be going well
for them. But one afternoon, the couple found themselves lying flat on
the floor of their home for two hours while soldiers outside fired con-
tinuous rounds of ammunition into the house.

When the soldiers left, after threatening to return that night,
Angelique and her husband knew they must run for their lives.
Pausing at the door, Angelique surveyed the shattered windows and
bullet-riddled walls. She said, "Whatever the Lord wants me to have,
He will restore to me." Then the couple hurriedly left.

They left, not knowing the whereabouts of their daughter and the
nephew they had raised as a son, or whether the two were even alive.
They left, knowing the soldiers would ransack and destroy what
remained of their house. They left with the clothes on their backs and
$60 cash. Later, they were robbed of the $60 at gunpoint.

For six months, the couple endured suffering, hunger, and terror.
They moved from place to place seeking safety. They ate hog feed and
wild grains. Near starvation, Angelique lost 30 pounds from an already
trim frame; her husband lost 50 pounds.

They witnessed brutal slayings of men, women, and babies. They
received word that Angelique's brother, his wife, and foster daughter
had been murdered by soldiers. They were with Angelique's father
when he died of a massive heart attack after hearing the news of his son.

Eventually, the couple was reunited with their daughter Andrea.
They grieved to learn their foster son had been killed.

Angelique was one of more than 1 million people whose lives
were shattered in a bloody, 18-month civil war in Liberia. Troops on
both sides of the conflict massacred civilians and looted villages. More
than 20,000 people died.

Over and over during those nightmare weeks, Angelique quoted
Scripture passages she had committed to memory: "The Lord is my
shepherd; I shall not want . . . Yea, though I walk through the valley
of the shadow of death, I will fear no evil: for thou art with me . . .
Surely goodness and mercy shall follow me all the days of my life."

Goodness and mercy? Over and over, Angelique cried, "Lord,
show me Your mercy! Where is Your mercy?" Along the way, she

caught glimmers of God's goodness. Finally, she began to experience the surging of His compassion again.

Fleeing the country, Angelique, Andrea, and Andrea's fiancé boarded a cargo ship to Guinea. (Angelique's husband had to stay behind since the paperwork allowing him to leave was not ready.) The ship was crammed with 400 people. What should have been a two-day journey turned into a six-day ordeal.

Though the vessel reached Guinea on schedule, the Guinean cabinet learned the next day that rebel soldiers were aboard and ordered the ship back to Liberia. By night, the refugees were pushed into the high seas without compass, anchor, or light. They remained outside the access channel for two long days, during which time Angelique gave her last bit of food to a dying child and her last water to an elderly woman.

Again, the ship docked in Guinea. Guinean soldiers unloaded the cargo. The next morning, authorities ordered the ship to leave for Liberia by noon, with all passengers still aboard. Amid appalling conditions and panicking people, Angelique and Andrea prayed intensely.

Then, a young man approached the ship. Pointing to Angelique, he told authorities, "That's my aunt." He was allowed to board the vessel and talk to Angelique. After asking her, "What can I do for you?" he promised, "I will let you off this ship."

The young man left, then returned later with the consul from the American embassy and a letter from the foreign minister. As a result, Angelique and her family walked off that vessel two hours before it was to leave for Liberia. They were the only Liberians allowed to disembark.

When asked about the young man, Angelique says, "I've never seen him before in my life. And I've never seen him since."

The End of the Tunnel

You've driven into a tunnel. To get to the other end, you must keep your seat behind the wheel; but your car must continue to move forward, and your headlights must continue to function.

If your headlights go out or if you begin feeling claustrophobic and try to jump from the car, you're in trouble. If you stop, turn off the engine, and wait, you will not reach the daylight again. And probably, an unsuspecting driver will rear-end you.

When you enter the dark tunnel of dashed hopes, remember that the tunnel does have another end. To get there, sit still . . . and keep moving.

Wait quietly for God to prove Himself strong in your behalf once more. Dwell on the fact that you will again see His great love poured out in abundance. Let the assurance of future good quiet your spirit.

But while you wait, don't park. While you "sit," keep your foot on the accelerator, your hands on the wheel, and your eyes on the guiding light of God's Word. Go toward God. Seek Him. Pursue knowing Him, loving Him, pleasing Him, growing in Him. No matter how dark things get, keep heading toward the Light.

Accept His Yoke

Almost nobody uses yokes these days, especially in the United States. Few people farm, and those who do generally use machinery to do the tasks animals once did.

But in Jeremiah's day, yokes were a common sight. They were the curved pieces of wood by which two draft animals were joined at the neck to enable them to work together.

The yoke indicated servitude. Once yoked, an animal served the one who placed the yoke on his neck.

Yokes were burdens borne for a purpose. No one yoked an animal only to leave it standing. Rather, the farmer placed the yoke on the animals to assist him in drawing a load or pulling a plow.

Finally, the yoke denoted companionship in the struggle. A "yoke of oxen" equals two oxen. Together, the animals tackled the task.

Reflecting on his own devastating, end-of-hope time, Jeremiah said, "It is good for a man to bear the yoke while he is young" (Lam. 3:27 NIV).

Jeremiah wasn't excited about the pain he was going through. But he realized people can emerge from the hard times one of two ways . . . bitter or better. He declared that the only way to emerge better is to accept the yoke.

God's yokes are not wooden, but they do indicate servitude. God hems or yokes us in ways we would rather He did not use. We can stiffen our necks and try to refuse His yokes, but in so doing we show ourselves unwilling to be His servants.

God's yokes always have purpose. He sees a task to be done, then He prepares those He intends to do that task. What He uses as preparation may seem useless catastrophe to human eyes; but the God of all wisdom and love knows what He is doing.

He never leaves us to bear the yoke alone. Jesus became a man so He could get into the harness with us. Since Christ's death and His resurrection, His Spirit lives within believers, enabling us to do what we otherwise could not.

Still, bearing the yoke is not pleasant. To accept the servitude, the purpose we usually cannot see, and the invisible companionship God promises, we must humble ourselves. Most of us would rather do anything than humble ourselves, especially when we understand what's involved.

• "Let him sit alone in silence, for the Lord has laid it on him," Jeremiah urged (Lam. 3:28 NIV). To humble yourself in the absence of breakthrough is to face the crisis uncomplaining. That does not mean you must bottle up all the anguish you feel. Jeremiah did plenty of complaining to the Lord. Yet before all those Jews to whom he could have said, "I told you so," he sat quietly. He did not confront them.

Pride would have been anything but silent in the situation. But Jeremiah refused to let pride have its way.

Like the prophet, you have freedom to speak your mind to God. Just remember that the One to Whom you speak is not answerable to you. He wants honesty; He requires worship and humility. Once you've had your say, He may or may not answer immediately. If you want to hear Him, you humble yourself by waiting quietly.

Moreover, you do not have freedom to air your feelings and complaints before anyone and everyone. When you humble yourself, you give up that right. You choose to sit silently until your Lord reveals to whom you may confide your distress.

• "Let him bury his face in the dust," said Jeremiah (Lam. 3:29a NIV). Not a very pleasing picture: God's prophet urging, "Eat dirt." But Jeremiah was trying to make a point. To put your mouth in the dust, it is almost essential that you lie flat.

In times of hopelessness, have you gotten flat on your face before God? Have you physically lain prostrate before Him? Have you been desperate enough to say, "Anything You do, Lord, is right. Anything you want from me, I'll give"? You humble yourself when every part of you bows in submission to your Lord.

• "Let him offer his cheek to one who would strike him, and let him be filled with disgrace" (Lam. 3:30 NIV). When all hope for a certain breakthrough ends, you will likely encounter some persons who feel they know exactly how you should have handled things . . . and are eager to tell you so. You may receive some slaps in the face, literally or otherwise. People may mock you, blame you, scorn you, or point fingers at you. You may live with a stigma. You may feel great shame.

Jeremiah said, "Let them do their worst. Don't retaliate." Impossible? No. The One whose Spirit lives in you took the sting of slaps and shame He did not deserve. He did not take up for Himself, but instead kept entrusting Himself to His heavenly Father. In fact, He humbled Himself to the point of death.

The same Christ can enable you not to retaliate, if you will humble yourself enough to let Him.

Accepting the Yoke in Bishkek
Recollections of Andrea Mullins, Continued

"On Saturday (the day we learned we had no Bibles), we had our first contact with the Russian Christians in Bishkek. We will never forget that on a Saturday afternoon they filled the church to overflowing in order to worship with us. The choir sang magnificently in a language we could not understand, but with a Spirit that revealed their love for God.

"As it turned out, we were with the believers for most of our time in Bishkek. We ate with them, worshiped with them, participated in a wedding ceremony and feast, took communion with them, preached in their churches, sang with them, and celebrated the harvest time with them. We were humbled by their commitment to the cause of Christ. They had so little, but what they wanted from us was not our possessions or our wealth. They wanted to know how to disciple to those whom they reach with the gospel. They wanted our prayers and our encouragement.

"We were the learners. They were the teachers as they revealed a steadfastness that had seen them through persecution and enabled them to survive in a Muslim republic. Even as they met with us, they told us they knew the time would soon come when the doors would be closed again. They want to reach the lost and disciple new believers while they can.

"Seeing the violent evidence of the Muslim faith and the Kirghiz believers' need for US Christians to help them prepare for the days ahead, I could not help but think that God had intervened in our plans. He knew the true priority for our ministry in Bishkek. He blessed us by taking our effort to follow Him and leading us in a better way.

"Yes, I still hunger to hand a Muslim Kirghiz the Word of God. I pray that we will reach them with the gospel. But if we can help the believers who live there to be the most effective church possible, then I will have handed the Bible to those people in a way that will be much more powerful and long-term.

"We do not know for sure why the Bibles were not available for us to give out in Kirghizia, but I do know that God used us and taught us through unique experiences. I thrilled to hear the warm and powerful greeting one of our young women brought in the worship service on Sunday afternoon and the message another young woman brought in another church that morning. I heard the beautiful blend of American and Russian voices singing 'Amazing Grace.' I experienced the emotional and powerful prayers of the *babushkas*, women who have kept the church alive and faithfully prayed for open doors for the gospel through generations. I felt the hugs, kisses, and love of my Christian sisters, who know what it means to forsake all for Christ. I was challenged to put away all the trappings I hold dear to encounter Christ in a way I have never met Him before.

"Yes, the plans we made were not realized, yet we saw God at work in Kirghizia."

Hope . . . and Faith and Love

Do oxen enjoy accepting the yoke? Possibly not. When it comes, they know the path ahead will be hard.

Accepting God's yoke may sometimes seem impossibly hard for you too. But if you do not accept it, you choose a way that is ultimately even harder. You choose the weed-choked way of bitterness, the plummeting path of hopelessness.

And if you do bear the yoke?

During the dark weeks when civil war claimed the lives of five of her family members, Angelique led daily prayertimes for those with whom she lived as refugee in their own country. A young businessman asked her, "How can you continue to lead prayer meetings with all these tragedies coming your way?"

She answered, "With faith, there is courage. With courage, one reflects on all the good things God permitted you to enjoy. Then, you have thanksgiving and a continued faith that God will restore unto you those things He wants you to have. At the end, you will see God's pure love."

8

CLOSING THE BREACHES

*"We always carry around in our body the death of
Jesus, so that the life of Jesus may also be
revealed in our body"
(2 Cor. 4:10 NIV).*

I pray I won't forget the faces of the Soviet people. Most looked as bleak as the Moscow weather we encountered during the last half of our visit there.

Except when we offered the New Testaments, we saw few smiles. Waitresses served us whole meals with unutterably somber faces. Although we grinned at them repeatedly and said please and thank you often, they would not show even a hint of a smile.

Everywhere we went, we saw hungry, searching eyes. When we stood to tell the truth about Jesus, listeners stood without moving as long as we talked.

A few faces in particular I know I'll remember.

•*Lyuda* accepted a Bible from me after our first evangelistic service on Red Square. Then, she asked me to sign it.

On the flyleaf of her New Testament I wrote, "John 3:16." I jotted the page number where the verse could be found, and I signed my name.

Lyuda, a young woman, was dark-haired, dark-skinned, and beautiful. She spoke some English, and she was eager to talk. She told me she had read "a little" of the Bible before. She also told me she was Arab, and a Muslim.

"Christians and Muslims have something in common," I told her. "We both believe Jesus lived; but we differ in our teachings about Jesus. This verse helps explain what Christians believe about Jesus."

I opened her Bible to John 3:16, circled it, and asked her to read it. She did. To my amazement, she broke into a broad smile and nodded enthusiastically. Before we parted company, Lyuda promised she would read her New Testament.

•I met *Vladimir* in Moscow. A blonde in his 20s, he spoke little English. I spoke almost no Russian, so we had difficulty communicating.

Vladimir told me, "I became a Christian just before the coup." Without any Russian-language helps, I tried to explain to him that he was now a spiritual baby who needed to grow by reading his Bible and finding a Bible-teaching church.

He laughed about being a baby. His responses to my other statements were surprisingly cynical coming, as I thought, from a new believer. Among other things, he kept saying, "The Bible is too hard to understand." I urged him to pray and ask God to help him understand.

Then, he told me, "I prayed for the first time before the coup."

That was when I realized: Vladimir had not accepted Christ. He had just begun to believe God might exist. He was searching, yet still cynical. He may have thought that since Christians pray, praying had made him a Christian. I had added to his confusion.

Soon afterward, I had to leave. I walked away feeling utterly frustrated. I had spent most of my brief time with Vladimir trying desperately to tell him the wrong thing. I prayed that God would somehow bring good out of the mess I'd made.

•*Sveta* would not look at me or any of the other missions team members who visited her eighth-grade class. The class was part of a government-run boarding school/orphanage in Moscow. As ten of us Americans stood in a line across the front of the small room, Sveta's classmates sat at their desks, smiling brightly at us. We talked to them; they talked to us through the teacher who translated.

Meanwhile, Sveta wandered around the back of the room. She picked up a book and flipped through it. Then she put the book away, climbed up on an empty back desk, and pulled an object off a top shelf. I don't remember exactly what she found, but she made a point to interest herself in it for a few minutes before climbing back up to put it away.

By that time, we had finished with the formal part of our visit to the classroom. We were free to roam around the room, mingling with the students.

I headed straight for Sveta. We exchanged names and the few Russian pleasantries I knew. Then, I opened my little black notebook and asked Sveta for her address. Grabbing the notebook, she took off across the room. She stopped beside her teacher, who was busy talking to someone else. Standing at the teacher's elbow, Sveta kept motioning me to wait.

I wondered what she was doing. Surely an eighth-grader knew how to write her own address. But when Sveta returned a few minutes later, I understood. She had gotten the teacher to write in English letters, rather than the Cyrillic alphabet used in Russian. She wanted to make sure I could read that address.

A team member took a picture of Sveta and me. I sent one copy to Sveta. I keep another copy near the place where I have my daily quiet time. It reminds me to pray for and write to a young lady who tried to act as though she didn't care . . . and won my heart.

Sveta, Vladimir, and Lyuda taught me truths I might have missed if I hadn't met them face-to-face. The peoples of the former Soviet Union have experienced a miraculous breakthrough outwardly. But most of those 290 million individuals still know nothing of inward breakthrough. Further, the disintegration of the old system has left gaping holes in their lives. Only God knows how they will fill the breaches.

One Cause for Reluctance

Sometimes God is doing His breakthrough work and you may not even realize it. In fact, you may hinder it because you're looking at breakthrough in terms of outward situations or other people, and in terms of yourself. You're looking for a visible, tangible change in "it" or "them." Meanwhile, God is seeking to work an invisible revolution in you.

Of course, there's a good reason you may want breakthrough to happen everywhere but in yourself. Breakthroughs leave holes.

A football team charging through a banner creates a gap. So does a baseball that shatters a window, or a wrecking ball that crashes through a wall. Bullets, knives, and needles can pierce flesh creating holes that we call *wounds*. They bleed.

Spiritual breakthroughs leave holes too. A person who turns abruptly to God may find that friends haven't turned. The person now has a gap in life which those friends once filled. Someone who conquers a destructive habit must deal with the big bare spot the habit formerly occupied.

You may hurt with others when a sudden change for the better leaves them wounded in some way. Still, you can probably deal with breakthroughs that leave holes in someone else. You may even encourage such breakthroughs. If a friend is trying to decide whether to have much needed minor surgery, for example, you may urge her to go on and get the matter taken care of.

If you face the same decision, you will almost always hesitate. You may even reject what everyone else agrees is the better choice. Why? Because few people accept something that will leave a hole in them.

For the same reason, you may have great difficulty agreeing to let God work breakthrough in you. To do so is to give Him permission to act in a way that can wound. You may hurt; you may bleed.

Why even consider saying yes to such a thing? Because in the spiritual realm, as in the physical, this saying is true: No pain, no gain. In his book *The Release of the Spirit*, Watchman Nee asserts that "the breaking of the outward man . . . must be accomplished before [God] can use us in an effective way."[1]

Nee uses the term "outward man" to describe not our physical bodies, but a part of us most people would call "inward," the part that is invisible, but not spirit. The Bible sometimes refers to it as the "old self." It includes the mind, emotions, and will.

If you have accepted Jesus as Lord, God's Spirit lives inside you. In fact, the Holy Spirit so permeates your spirit that it is impossible to tell where one leaves off and the other begins.

God's Spirit is the Spirit of life. Hence, God's life dwells in you. But God desires that His life do more than sit within; He intends His life to flow out.

However, His life cannot flow out from you when your "outer man" dams the flow. According to Nee, your mind, will, and emotions, still bent in the old ways, form an encasing shell around the spirit. Until you allow God to shoot holes in the thoughts, feelings, and decisions that come from *you* rather than from *Him*, you cannot be an outlet for Him. His life stays imprisoned within. Nee continues, "This is an invariable spiritual fact! Our spirit is released according to the degree of our brokenness."[2]

Two Pictures of Released Life

Songs have been written and sermons preached about the woman in Mark 14 who brought an alabaster vial of costly perfume to Jesus. Until the woman broke the vial, she could not pour the sweet ointment on her Lord.

Nee and others see in this episode a picture of our need for brokenness before God. We believers are "the aroma of Christ." Through us God "spreads everywhere the fragrance of the knowledge of him" (2 Cor. 2:14 NIV).

Yet Nee warns that too often, instead of releasing the fragrance, we treasure the box. We cater to our own desires and feelings, admire our own talents, cherish our own wisdom, and choose our own way.

Gideon marched against a formidable army of Midianites with only 300 men. By night, the 300 surrounded the enemy camp. Each man held a trumpet and an empty pitcher with a torch inside it. On signal, all were to blow the trumpets, smash the pitchers, hold high the torches, and cry, "For the Lord and for Gideon!" The 300 did as commanded, and routed the vast Midianite army.

What if, while waiting for the signal, the men had begun examining their pitchers? What if they had decided the workmanship was too good to waste? What if they had not broken what God had said to break? The sound of the shattering, as well as the sudden appearance of the light, worked to throw the enemy into confusion and to accomplish God's plans. Remember: the men held the light the whole time; but only when the pitchers were shattered could the light effectively pierce the darkness.

Paul said believers carry the light of the glory of God in "jars of clay." The "jars" are our bodies. How does the light get out? "We are hard pressed on every side . . . perplexed . . . persecuted . . . struck down. We always carry around in our body the death of Jesus, so that the life of Jesus may also be revealed in our body" (2 Cor. 4:8-10 NIV).

As God does His shattering work in us, the light is released.

Three Evidences of Unbrokenness

You can choose to avoid being shattered. You can sidestep God's breaking and yet continue to do most of the things Christians are supposed to do. You can pray unbroken, preach and teach unbroken, and do good deeds unbroken; but your life and service for God will be as effective as an unplugged power saw. You may hack your way through each day's duties, but you will wear yourself out in the process. And, in spite of all your effort, you will not be able to please the Lord or minister His life to others.

How do you know whether you are broken or unbroken?

1. *The unbroken lack power.* You may have error-free theology, live by high moral standards, and do good deeds often. But when you speak or minister to someone in Jesus' name, does everyone (including you) come away feeling flat?

The words may be right, but they are dusty. They do not breathe with God's life. They don't explode into others' spirits with the insight, rebuke, challenge, or encouragement intended. The deeds may seem nice, but they don't result in changed lives.

You may want desperately to operate in God's power. You may know the term *brokenness* and even teach it. You may think yourself spiritually broken. But here's the litmus test question: Are you a channel for God's power?

If the "spiritual" things you say and do sit becalmed, unable to reach others, take note. When you are broken, your words and deeds will ride into the lives both of believers and unbelievers on the tidal wave of God's life.

2. *The unbroken lack insight.* Paul told the Corinthians they were looking at things as they were outwardly. Every believer makes that mistake from time to time. But if you have not been broken, you can look at things *only* from the outside. You see, hear, taste, smell, and touch. Based on that sensory input, you make decisions according to your reasonings, feelings, and desires.

You pray, but not knowing how to listen for God's answer, you have to figure out what His answer appears to be. You have "the mind of Christ," but that mind is locked in the tower, so to speak.

If you've been broken, you can see past the visible; you can hear the unhearable. You don't dismiss your senses or your ability to think or feel, but you view all that input in a different light. God's Spirit unleashed in you rearranges all the data and puts it together in a way you could not do on your own.

3. *The unbroken lack pliability.* If you always know best, you're unbroken. If you secretly delight in patting yourself on the back, you're unbroken. If you're "set in your ways"; if you're unwilling to release

any one area of your life to God; if your words and actions tend to divide rather than unify the believers, you're unbroken.

Do others detect in you an undercurrent of pride? Do you come across to them as hard, sharp, and unyielding? Do people hesitate to approach you? Do they find you transparent or opaque?

Can you receive ideas from others and count those ideas really worthwhile? Can you receive help or instruction when it is offered? Can you confess your sins readily? Will you let people see you cry?

If you are a leader, you may feel you are not supposed to yield. You may think you are to head out, and those under your authority are to follow. You may believe that if others question your direction, they are tampering with the will of God. Even if you are not in a leadership role, you may feel your choices, words, and actions are nobody else's business.

But God has made His people one body. Though leaders are to lead, they are first to love. All believers are to be knit together under Christ's headship. Whether making decisions, carrying out tasks, or dealing with problems, we function best in harmony with other believers.

Once broken, you will be pliable, like a thread in the master weaver's hands. You will no longer remain stiff with pride or obstinacy. You'll allow God to interweave your life with others'. You'll be willing to learn even from "babes." You'll touch and feel the needs of those around you. You'll move as one with the fabric of Christ's church.

Two Ways God Breaks Us

God is seeking to do His breaking work in you each time you meet suffering, trial, or hindrance. He does not necessarily send such things, but He orders and uses them to apply pressure to the areas of your life that He knows remain unbroken before Him.

Watchman Nee calls this work God's "discipline." Nee says, "This is the discipline of the Holy Spirit: when all kinds of things and all sorts of people are pressing in from all directions."[3]

The breaking happens in two ways. (1) Daily trials knock the props out from under you one by one, forcing you to rely on God in each area of your life. (2) Somewhere along the way, one thorough breaking crushes your self-will and creates a spirit of brokenness.

A Thorough Breaking

For most of his Christian life, Larry had felt that Christianity had to offer more than he had received. He'd read John 14:12 where Jesus said, "I am telling you the truth: whoever believes in me will do what I do—yes, he will do even greater things" (TEV). Larry had prayed, "Lord, I would sure like to do these greater things." Yet, he never did. The verse haunted and seemed to condemn him. He wanted to believe the promise, but didn't know how it could happen.

Someone looking at Larry's life would not have believed he felt he didn't measure up spiritually. Larry grew up deeply involved in church activities. Along the way, he had a genuine conversion experience and during his teen years, became a leader among the youth of his church.

After graduating from college, Larry taught high school math for one year, then he and his wife packed up what little they had and took off for seminary.

Three years later, the couple moved to Pennsylvania to pastor a new church of 17 members. After several years at that church and then several more years at a church in Kentucky, Larry and Marie set out to minister and witness in Hong Kong.

All this time, Larry was serving the Lord as fully as he knew how. "Yet, at the same time," he says, "there was something inside of me that just was leaving me extremely empty."

The emptiness began to come to a head when Larry and his family relocated to an island in Hong Kong where they planned to start a new church. Not long ago, the island of Tsing-Yi was a fishing village with just over 1,000 people. Now it has a mushrooming population in the hundreds of thousands.

On Tsing-Yi, Larry felt a great sense of helplessness, though he had both the training and experience needed to start a church. "Lord, I don't know how to do this," he prayed.

He began teaching English to older high school students. A few students enrolled in a Bible study he led in his home. As he taught them and worked to start the church, Larry felt God was working, not *through* him, but *in spite of* him. His efforts didn't make any inroads. The things he'd been trained to do didn't seem to be paying off. Yet, God was moving, using other ways and means.

Meanwhile, the students began to ask Larry questions. "If I become a Christian, what will your God do for me?" they queried.

Larry answered as he had been trained, "Wouldn't it be nice to know that when you die you're going to go to heaven and you can have eternal life?" He also assured the youth that God would answer their prayers.

The students shot back, "If I pray about something, will your God do something immediately to help me? Will He help me make better grades at school?"

Larry could only reply, "Well, He could help you to study, but we couldn't promise you the results." His answers didn't satisfy him or them. He says, "It bothered me deeply that I didn't have the answers to the questions they were asking."

Then, five of the high school students in Larry's Bible study went on the equivalent of a senior trip to Taiwan. Before they left, one girl named Mandy came by Larry's house to tell him, "I want you to know I'm going away for ten days with some of my friends. When I get back, I want to talk with you some more about Jesus and about your God."

But Mandy didn't get back. She and three others of the five were killed in a hotel fire in Taiwan. Larry was devastated. He kept asking, "Why, God? They were so close to coming to know You."

The tragedy, combined with Larry's inability to answer unbelievers' heartfelt questions, his sense of helplessness in a new situation, and his feeling that what he was doing was out of sync with what God was doing, brought Larry to a new low one summer. He says, "I got to a point that I found it difficult even to pray. I didn't want to pray. The only time I would read the Bible was in preparation for a sermon. I was so miserable. I was wanting something, but I didn't know what it was. And I didn't know where to find it."

In August Larry received a phone call from Tom, a friend living in Korea. Tom told Larry, "I want to come to Hong Kong to see you."

Larry had known Tom for a number of years. He said, "Tom, something's happened. Your voice has changed. I can tell by your whole mannerism something has happened to you."

Tom answered, "Yes, I want to tell you about it. That's why I want to come to Hong Kong."

In September, Tom and his wife and family flew to Hong Kong. Larry met them at the airport. When he saw Tom, Larry said, "Tom, you even look different. Something's happened in your life. You've got to tell me. I've been on this search. I've been so miserable as a Christian. I just don't know what to do."

That afternoon, Tom and Larry talked. During the conversation Tom asked Larry, "Have you ever read the book *Release of the Spirit* by Watchman Nee?"

"No," Larry answered. "A couple of years ago somebody sent me that book, but I haven't read it yet."

Tom said, "Let me encourage you to read it."

Later that day, Larry took Tom and his family to the hotel where they had asked to stay. Then, Larry went home hungry for God to act. He prayed: God, You're going to have to do this because I don't know what to do; I don't know how to do it. And, God, I'm willing to accept whatever way You want to do it. I'm willing to accept whatever You want to reveal to me, whatever You want to show me is wrong.

No one else was home. Larry went immediately to his library, picked up the book Tom had recommended, and began to read. He says, "It was almost as if the book had been written just for me."

That afternoon, Larry had what he describes as "the major breakthrough that caught me in every area of my life."

"God began to empty me," he says. "It was almost like watching a videotape of my past life and God taking me through frame by frame and showing me all the areas where I had trusted in my own knowledge and my own self. I had been doing so much for so long in the flesh, and I hadn't realized it.

"I would confess and agree with God as He would show me each frame. Sometimes, I would try to hurry on, and God would say, 'No, there's more in that picture frame I want to show you.' So I began to learn to wait on Him and to let Him do that."

When the afternoon ended Larry felt that in a sense, he had been machine-gunned. He'd spent his life serving the Lord. Now, all the works he'd tried to do for God lay in the dust, shot full of holes.

Yet, Larry no longer felt at the end of himself. Rather, he felt the joy of a new beginning. He had experienced breakthrough. For the next six weeks, he closed the breaches with extended periods of prayer, sometimes spending four to six hours a day praying.

"It wasn't that I was scheduling the times," he says. "I just knew that the Lord wanted me to be with Him at certain times, and it didn't matter what time of the day or night it would happen."

During Larry's extended prayertimes, he continued to recognize many things other than God in which he had placed his trust. Also, God reminded him of people he needed to forgive and sins he needed to confess.

Larry says, "One of the great things I learned was how to sit quietly before the Lord. I could spend up to 45 minutes, even an hour, and not say anything and just enjoy the presence of the Lord." Then, instead of rattling off his own list of prayer requests, Larry would ask God to direct his petitions.

It's Better to Be with God

Larry came away from that six-week period convinced of two truths that were, for him, life-changing. First, he'd learned that it's far better to be with God than to do things for Him.

All his Christian life, Larry had been setting his priorities the opposite way. Believing many other Christians make the same mistake, Larry says, "I hear over and over from pastors and other church leaders how they're becoming weary of all the programs and activities of the church, and they're not really seeing results. God has shown me that results come from being with Him, not from our activity."

Larry adds, "I began to slow down." While decreasing his activity, Larry increased time spent with the Lord. He began learning to listen to Him. During this period, Larry's church began growing. Four months after its beginning, attendance at services was running in the 70s, a remarkable start for a Hong Kong congregation.

One day Adam, a missionary from another area, asked Larry the secret of such a successful church start. Larry told him, "What has helped us to grow more than anything has been prayer. We're really learning how to pray and to let the Lord lead us in our prayer."

Adam replied, "Well, I know that. But what else did you do?"

Larry says, "I kept trying to explain that it was really through prayer. He just couldn't get over it." Finally, Adam asked, "Well, how much time do you pray anyway?"

At that point, Larry was still in the six-week period after his breakthrough. He said, "What I'm doing right now is not normal in comparison to what I've done the rest of my life. I pray anywhere from four to six hours a day."

At first, Adam didn't know whether or not to believe Larry. But once convinced that he was telling the truth Adam asked, "Don't you feel you're cheating on your other responsibilities by spending so much time praying?"

Adam's questions reminded Larry how foreign his new way of thinking is from the thinking of many believers. Adam's concerns reminded Larry of his own views before being broken. Something else reminded Larry of himself before breakthrough too.

Adam confided, "I don't know why I'm going to tell you this. I'm about ready to resign. Even my wife doesn't know. I'm miserable in my own life and experience. I don't know what's happened to you, and I'm not sure I can understand it all, but I sure wish something like that would happen to me."

Larry responded by praying with Adam for breakthrough to occur in his life.

Christ Is My Life

Larry learned a second thing from his six weeks spent closing the breaches. His identity as a person lay not in what he did or titles he had, but only in his relationship to Christ.

Before being broken, Larry had never understood the work of the Holy Spirit in a believer's life. Afraid of being a fanatic, he'd held God's Spirit at arm's length. As pastors and seminary professors taught him, he built his ministry on what he had learned. But when he began to affirm, "Christ is my life," God convicted him how little he had ever let Christ's Spirit be his teacher. He had failed not only to learn what the Spirit wanted to teach him but also to receive and exercise the gifts the Spirit gives.

When Larry began to listen to the Holy Spirit, "The Word of God literally became alive in my life" he says. He began to understand how to answer questions that had previously baffled him.

Now when students ask, "What would your God do for me?" Larry tells them, "God can set you free from whatever problems you may have." He says, "Many times, God has revealed to me what their problems are, and we're able to pray together and see people set free."

For example, a Christian doctor came to Larry during a recent three-day retreat. "I'd like for you to pray for me," the doctor said. He told Larry about a couple of problem areas in his life. Since being broken, Larry has learned that when people name their needs, they may miss the area that's most important.

He said, "Let's pray together and ask God if there's any area He may want to reveal to you." As the two prayed, Larry saw a mental picture of a young boy about five years old filled with great fear. He asked the doctor, "When you were about five or six years old, what was your home life situation? What was the environment?"

The doctor replied, "Oh, I was quite happy. There weren't any problems. I always remember that being a very good time in my life."

Larry said, "I don't know why, but I'm sensing that as a young boy you must have been afraid of something. Was there something you were afraid of?"

Tears welled up in the doctor's eyes and ran down his cheeks. He said, "I've never told anybody this, but I feared my father. He was a very condemning man. I could never do anything to please him."

Larry asked him, "Do you know why God may have wanted you to remember this?"

After praying with Larry a little longer, the doctor said, "I've been looking at God like I have my father." In his medical studies and other areas of his life, the doctor had felt God was punishing him or condemning him any time he did less than perfect.

As a result of his prayertime with Larry, the doctor forgave his father for treating him so harshly. He asked God's forgiveness for the unforgiving attitude he had carried toward his father for so long. Perhaps most important, he saw his heavenly Father in a new light. He was freed from his image of a condemning God and was able to receive His Lord's unconditional love.

In Christ, God has given Larry a "gift of knowledge." Since being broken, Larry has found new ability to use that gift to minister through prayer and counseling. When the Lord shows Larry something about someone that he could not otherwise have known, he feels very keenly his responsibility to handle that knowledge wisely.

He says, "I've seen a lot of healing take place in people's lives. I've seen people come to know the Lord."

One woman came forward during her third visit to Larry's church to say that she had been living under great stress for over a year.

Later that week, when Larry visited her, she told him, "Your God is such a great and mighty God. Ever since you prayed for me, I have had more peaceful rest at night than I have had in over a year. I can't thank you and your God enough for what He did for me."

Larry told her, "Well, actually, He wants to do much more than that. But He can't because He's on the outside and He wants to come in to be on your inside."

She said, "Well then, I want Him on the inside. How do I get Him to the inside of me?"

Within a few minutes, the woman was praying to receive Christ. Larry says, "We've seen great changes take place in this woman's life. And three of her children have received Christ."

The Outpouring of God's Life

Every experience of brokenness is unique. Just as each believer has a different testimony regarding salvation, each believer whom God has broken has a different story to tell. Circumstances that would bring you to the breaking point may not bear the least resemblance to those that led to Larry's breaking.

But as with every true salvation experience, each occasion of major brokenness has a common thread. In salvation, the thread is the inpouring of God's life as a result of surrender to the risen Lord Jesus. In brokenness, the thread is the outpouring of God's life when, as Larry says, "the Spirit of God comes upon us in a very special way and suddenly overpowers us."

Larry adds, "You don't have to wait until you're 40 years old to have this major breakthrough. In fact, I encourage you not to do that. Learn to come before the Lord and let Him deal with you."

Daily Difficulties

Once broken, you can't just relax for the rest of your days and let God's life flow. Sin and self will soon begin to dam up the holes God created to give Himself an outlet in you. To keep the way open, the Lord will do smaller breaking works through the daily trials, problems, and hurts you encounter. Like many believers, you may see the difficulties, but not see God's hand in them.

Yet, if you'll let Him, God will use all that seems hard in your life to deal with specific areas where inner breakthrough is still needed. The process will continue as long as you live on this earth. At different times, it will touch different areas.

The nonmoving checkout line, the slow car ahead, the train that always seems to cross your path when you have least time to spare may be God's instruments to break your impatience. Physical problems may signal His thrust to break bad health habits.

He may use pressure cooker situations to break you of worry, frightening situations to break you of fear, embarrassing situations to break you of pride.

Watchman Nee declares, "Whatever the things to which you are bound, God will deal with them one after another . . . He will not neglect one area in your life."[4]

A Child's Illness

I had been asked to write a one-year daily prayer guide, to be published in monthly installments. I was to travel to Birmingham, Alabama, a three-hour drive from my home, for two days of training. I made arrangements for Megan, our first-grader, to go to a neighbor's house both days after school and stay until Jerry got off work.

A Birmingham friend named Mary Ann offered to take care of four-year-old Amanda during my training. Mary Ann had a three-and-one-half-year-old daughter herself. We both thought the girls would enjoy playing together.

Not long after all the plans were made, a flu epidemic hit. It swept through Birmingham and into towns and cities nearer us. It raged through one school system in our county and then through the school Megan attended. The Monday before I was to leave on Thursday, Megan reported as she hopped in the car after school, "Eleven people were absent from my class today. Only 13 were there."

My heart sank. My stomach had been in a knot ever since the epidemic started. What if one or both of the girls got the flu just at the time for me to leave town? I'd have to stay home, of course. Yet, a number of very busy women had arranged their schedules to work with me those two particular days.

I prayed about the matter a lot that week. And every time I did, I believed God was telling me I would go to Birmingham at the set time. I tried to relax.

Then, on Wednesday morning, Megan woke up with the flu. Everyone, including our pediatrician's nurse and the mothers of several children who were just getting over the flu, told me how high Megan's fever would be during the initial stages. "Between doses of medicine, you'll probably have to keep her in the tub for three days to try to keep the fever down," the nurse said.

Amanda and I were scheduled to leave first thing the next morning. I would have to cancel the trip, wouldn't I?

It wasn't the first time I had faced a major decision over whether to leave a sick child to fulfill an out-of-town commitment. The first time, Megan was one year old. I had committed to teach women for a week at a denominational assembly in New Mexico. We lived in Tennessee.

About a month before the trip, Megan got sick with what appeared to be the 24-hour stomach flu. She recovered, and then, abruptly, the sick stomach recurred. For a solid month, she repeated the pattern: get sick at her stomach; spend several days slowly regaining her strength and her ability to eat; get sick all over again. Because she was able to keep down so little food, my normally very happy, very active baby lay listless most of the time.

During those weeks, I took Megan to the doctor three times. Extensive testing showed no physical cause for the problem. My trip to New Mexico was drawing alarmingly closer. Yet how could I leave my child sick?

One night, unable to sleep, I took my Bible, went to the den, sat down, and told the Lord I was going to stay there until I knew what He wanted me to do. I prayed and read until 3:00 in the morning. Finally, a verse in Isaiah 54 jumped off the page at me: "If anyone fiercely assails you it will not be from Me. Whoever assails you will fall because of you" (Isa. 54:15 NASB).

God used that verse to assure me Megan's illness was not "from Him." Her stomach problems were *not* His way of telling me not to go; rather, they were Satan's way of trying to block me from going. I realized that if I gave in to the devil's fierce assaults, I would be practically inviting him to make Megan sick every time he wanted to stop me from ministering. I called several prayer partners and asked them to claim Isaiah 54:15 with me.

Megan got sick at her stomach again about three days before I was to leave for New Mexico. The morning I boarded the airplane, I sent her to my parents' house looking pale and lethargic. By the time I reached my destination, she was somewhat better. Each day I was gone, she improved a bit more. I came home to a happy, bouncy little girl. The mysterious illness never recurred.

Five years later, Megan was sick again, this time with the flu. Once more, I needed to discern God's will. I knew His saying "Go" on a previous occasion didn't necessarily mean He was saying the same thing now. As I prayed, I wondered if I was wrong even to ask God what I should do. Maybe, this time, the illness *was* His way of telling me not to go.

I could not picture myself going. Wouldn't Megan feel abandoned if I walked out when she was so sick? And what would others think about my leaving? I knew the answer to that; many would think I was not a fit mother. It would seem to everyone that I was putting my ministry to women before my ministry to my child.

Yet somewhere beneath all the confusion, I kept sensing that God wanted me to go to Birmingham. Two things happened early in the day Wednesday that made me believe I might be on track.

First, when I told Jerry that Megan was sick, he volunteered to take care of her while I was away. To do that, he would have to take precious time off from his job. I highly valued the offer.

Then, I called Mary Ann. I told her the situation. I explained that Amanda was not sick but that she had been exposed to the flu. I asked, "Do you have any hesitation about my coming on and bringing Amanda?"

"No," Mary Ann answered immediately.

All day Wednesday (between Megan's almost constant calls for "Mama"), I prayed. "Father, You know I couldn't go if Jerry hadn't encouraged it. I couldn't go if Mary Ann had hesitated even a bit when I told her the situation. You've opened both those doors. And crazy as it sounds, I believe You're telling me to go.

"But, please, Father, I need one more confirmation. I just do not feel I can leave Megan with an extremely high fever. Please, if you want me to go, don't let her fever get to 102 degrees."

I also prayed, "Father, can I ask why You might want me to go on to Birmingham? Could you give me a Scripture verse that might explain what You're doing here?"

Wednesday evening about 6:00, Megan's fever dropped from 101 degrees, where it had hovered most of the day, to 99 degrees. It stayed down through the night.

Tucking her in that night, I noticed the Scripture plaque hanging above her bed. I had bought it shortly after she was born. It read: "For this child I prayed; and the Lord hath given me my petition which I asked of Him: Therefore also I have lent her to the Lord; as long as she liveth she shall be lent to the Lord" (1 Sam. 1:27-28 KJV).

The next morning, the car was packed and Amanda and I were ready to head out the door when I tiptoed into Megan's room to tell her good-bye. "We're going on to Birmingham," I said. "But Daddy will be here. I'll be calling to check on you. And Amanda and I will be back tomorrow evening.

"Megan," I continued, "I want you to know why I'm going. I've prayed and prayed about what to do. And I believe God wants me to trust *Him* to take care of you. I've told Him ever since you were born that you belong to Him, and I think this is one chance He's giving me to prove it."

She nodded. I couldn't tell if she really understood. I kissed her, walked out of the house, and drove off to Birmingham.

Megan had the flu a full week. But during the two days I was gone, her temperature never got over 99 degrees. She felt far better those two days than she did the following four.

Just as amazing, Amanda didn't get the flu. While I trained, she had a wonderful time playing with a new friend.

God used a rather commonplace occurrence, a child's illness, to do a breaking work in my life. What I feared the worst happened, and He turned it to good. Along the way, He broke through the fear, the pride, even the rational thinking that would have kept me from seeing His mighty hand work.

Four Options: What Do You Do with the Holes?

Holes cry to be filled. Spiritual holes cry to be filled with God Himself. Having experienced thorough brokenness before God, Paul said, "I have been crucified with Christ and I no longer live, but Christ lives in me" (Gal. 2:20*a* NIV). Meeting the discipline of daily difficulties, he said, "I die every day" (1 Cor. 15:31*a* NIV).

Paul let God do His breaking work. Then, he let God fill every breach with *His* life. When God sets out to do His breaking work in you, you can respond one of at least four ways.

Live with the Holes

Babylon had conquered Judah and carried her people away captive. Seventy years later, the first group of Jewish exiles made their way back to Jerusalem. After another 80 years, Ezra led a second group to return. By Nehemiah's day, returned Jews had been trying to reestablish life in Canaan for nearly 100 years, yet they still lived in fear and disgrace. Hostile peoples around them dominated them.

Why? Because the wall of Jerusalem still lay in ruins. Gaping holes left the city open to attack. The Jews knew of the holes, of course. Jerusalem's people well realized how vulnerable the breaches left them. But they assumed they would just have to live with those devastating gaps. They saw no possibility of rebuilding the wall. Until Nehemiah came on the scene.

Sveta, Vladimir, and Lyuda have never surrendered their lives to the Lord Jesus. As a result, each has a void within that can be filled only by Him. But until someone tells them different, they may assume the emptiness is just something they have to live with.

Many Christians, feeling the pain of their trials, set themselves simply to tolerate life. They believe the best they can do is "get by." They've not recognized that all the empty, aching places are holes the Holy Spirit can and will fill if they will just let Him.

Are you living with holes God created so that He could fill them?

Complain about the Holes

Author Watchman Nee says, "Each disciplinary working of the Holy Spirit has but one purpose: to break our outward man so that our inward man may come through. Yet here is our difficulty: we fret over trifles, we murmur at small losses. The Lord is preparing a way to use us, yet scarcely has His hand touched us when we feel unhappy, even to the extent of quarreling with God and becoming negative in our attitude."[5]

Do you respond to God's breaking work by complaining? Murmuring never closed a breach.

Patch the Holes

God wants to fill you. Yet, by trying to plug the "holes" in your life with everything and anything but Him, you may squirm away from the work of breakthrough He longs to accomplish.

Larry Harris tells of a young woman who is a leader among the single adults in her church. During a time of prayer with her, Larry asked, "Have you been crying a lot recently?" He says, "Tears started to trickle down her cheeks, and she said, 'Yes, how did you know?'

"I said, 'I didn't. I just sensed the Lord prompting me with that. Can you tell me what it's about?'"

The young woman told Larry about the stress and pressure she had at work. She said that her prayer life had become very sporadic and that when she did try to pray, her prayers seemed empty. Larry told her, "God really wants to bring healing through your life."

He says, "The sad thing was that, even as I spoke with her, she kept fighting back the tears and not really wanting to let go. She said, 'You know, I really want God to do something, but I'm too busy.'"

You too may want God to do something, *but* . . . if He is trying and you are patching, know that whatever you use to try to replace utter surrender to Him will not hold long. If you keep fighting Him, you may one day break, not in a way that allows His fragrance to flow out, but in a way that leaves you devastated.

Let God Fill the Holes

God's Holy Spirit alone can fill the gaps God's breaking creates. Nothing manmade can effectively plug them. You allow both the breakthrough and the closing of the breaches when, like Larry, you say, "God, I offer myself to You. I'm willing to accept whatever way You want to work."

Inner breakthroughs are easy to miss. They bring pain you may want to avoid. But personal brokenness before God is by far the most revolutionary type of breakthrough. It is by far the most rewarding. It is, in fact, a matter of death—and life.

9

LEARNING FROM BREAKTHROUGH

"So the three mighty men broke through the Philistine lines, drew water from the well near the gate of Bethlehem and carried it back to David. But he refused to drink it; instead, he poured it out before the Lord"
(2 Sam. 23:16 NIV).

I stood on a cardboard box in front of people I'd never seen before. They spoke a language different from mine. We were a world apart in terms of both geography and culture.

That day I stood among them, but could not claim to be one of them. I had no credentials. I had not experienced what they had. I could not even make myself understood without an interpreter.

They had no reason to stop and listen to me . . . except for the emptiness in their hearts and the hunger in their eyes. By their very intensity, they begged for a crust of bread. What joy! I could offer them the Bread of life.

It was Thursday, September 5. The Enterprisers were conducting an evangelistic street service on Red Square. Loaded with as many Russian New Testaments as we could carry, we had trudged to a spot near Lenin's tomb.

While soldiers watched from a distance and people who were crossing the square gathered, we sang in English, "Victory in Jesus" and "I Love to Tell the Story." The crowd continued to grow as Kathy, a young woman from Wyoming, brought greetings. Then, I stepped up on the box of Bibles we were using as a stand.

I scanned the faces of the men, women, and young people who had gathered. What I was about to say would fly in the face of everything they had ever been taught. Taking a deep breath, I began.

"The God we serve is Creator of heaven and earth," I said. "He is true. He is almighty. The Bible reveals Him." After each sentence, I paused to let Alla, one of our tour guides, translate. Alla was not a Christian. She was a Russian Jew.

As Alla and I spoke on one side of the Kremlin wall, a large red sign on the other side of the wall announced, Extraordinary Congress of People's Deputies. While the Enterprisers stood on Red Square calling people to Christ and offering them God's Word, the Soviet Congress was meeting to dismantle the Soviet Union itself.

History Lesson

Drastic change rocked Russia. It was 1917, and Russia included most of what later became the Soviet Union. Czar Nicholas II reigned. Indeed, Nicholas was the last in a long line of czars who had ruled Russia for nearly 400 years.

The first czar, Ivan IV, was crowned in 1547. Brutal, extremely suspicious, and perhaps a bit insane, Ivan formed a special police force and began a reign of terror. He had hundreds of aristocrats murdered and their estates turned over to landowners who served in the army and government. As Ivan burned many towns and villages, he killed church leaders who opposed him. He created a system of serfdom in Russia while serfdom, or the binding of peasants to the land, was disappearing in western Europe. The czars who followed Ivan continued to rule harshly. Some carried out limited reforms, but all maintained their own total power.

From time to time, revolutionary movements arose and were crushed—until March 1917. That month, the Russian people revolted. Nicholas II and his family were imprisoned and later killed. A provisional government was set up.

The temporary government lasted about eight months. On November 7, a man named Vladimir Lenin led a takeover. Under his leadership, workers and Bolshevik soldiers seized the Winter Palace in St. Petersburg, headquarters of the provisional government. By November 15, the Bolsheviks had taken Moscow.

Soon, Lenin was dictator of a new Communist state. For a short time, peasants seized much of the farmland, workers controlled factories, and both played important roles in Soviet councils. But the government tightened control, took over the industries, and forced the peasants to give up most of their products. To secure his rule, Lenin formed a secret police force.

Stalin, the next dictator, reintroduced serfdom by forcing most of the country's peasants onto collective farms. Millions of the more prosperous farmers were exiled to Siberia.

In the mid-1930s, Stalin began a program of terror. Neighbors and family members spied on one another. The secret police arrested millions, most of whom were later shot or sent to labor camps. Many Communist party heads were tried for "crimes against the people," eliminated, and replaced with young leaders Stalin could trust. Everything published, taught, or publicly spoken was controlled.

The dictators who followed Stalin continued to rule harshly. Some carried out limited reforms, but all maintained their own total power—until August 1991.

Do you begin to detect a pattern? By January 1992 the Soviet Union no longer existed. A provisional government had been set up. Market rate prices were being introduced into an already ailing Russian economy. Discontent in the new Commonwealth's different states threatened to lead to takeover.

Entrenched in the Same Rut?

After the August coup, I longed to broadcast an urgent warning to all the peoples of the former Soviet republics: "Any system created by man can be corrupted. Don't run to methods equally bad, or worse, in a desperate attempt to make things better. Seek answers in Him Who alone is the way, the truth, and the life." But even if I could somehow have captured the attention of those 290 million people, I wonder how many would have listened?

Now don't be too quick to shake your head. Like those who crushed czardom to create communism, we too are prone to repeat our mistakes. Something in human nature persists in finding new ways to entrench in the same old rut. If you're not careful, even the most major breakthrough will ultimately find you singing yet another verse of the same song.

You can encounter breakthrough, have a shouting time, and then fail to learn from what you've experienced. Or you can take time to ponder what has happened, let the lessons sink in, and by God's grace leap out of the rut and into new paths.

Lesson of the Bethlehem Well

King David made the latter choice. He learned from breakthrough. While enemy Philistines were camped in the valley of Rephaim, David was holed up in his stronghold, the cave of Adullam.

Does the scene sound familiar? Yes, the Philistines occupied the same valley and David occupied the same cave as when David prayed and God led him to breakthrough in battle against the Philistines. But this is another story, although it may have happened in the same time frame. This story is brief, but it's told twice in the Old Testament (2 Sam. 23 and 1 Chron. 11). The repetition itself indicates that God believes the account is worth noting.

It was summer. The Philistines had established their garrison in Bethlehem, David's hometown. During hot, dry days spent in the cave hiding and preparing for battle, David began to think about the water he used to drink from the Bethlehem well. Before long, he wanted that water so badly he could taste it. Finally, he blurted out, "How I wish someone would bring me a drink of water from the well by the gate at Bethlehem!" (2 Sam. 23:15 TEV).

Three of David's chief soldiers decided to get David's drink of water for him. They "broke through" the Philistine camp, drew some water from the well, and took it to David.

Did David do a dance, shout a bit, hug the men's necks, and gratefully drink that water? No. King David poured the water out on the ground.

Was David an ungrateful wretch? No. He meant well. While dumping the precious liquid, he prayed, "Lord, I could never drink this! It would be like drinking the blood of these men who risked their lives!" (2 Sam. 23:17 TEV).

Then, was David's thinking faulty? Did his symbolic gesture undercut his men's courage, sacrifice, and purpose in going? In refusing the water, did he unwittingly rob the three of the appropriate thanks due them?

It might seem so, but I don't believe so. I believe David's reaction showed he had learned at least four vital lessons from the break-through at the Philistine camp.

Truth 1: His craving was not harmless.

It seemed innocent enough for a thirsty soldier to want water from his hometown well; but Bethlehem wasn't "home" anymore for David. For the time being, in fact, the town lay in enemy hands. David couldn't honestly claim the water as his until he could retake the town.

And the thought, *It would be nice to have some of that water*, didn't just cross David's mind. It camped there. In fact, David "had a craving" (2 Sam. 23:15a NASB).

The Hebrew word translated "craving" in that verse is the same term rendered "set your desire" in the tenth commandment: "'You shall not covet. . . . You shall not set your desire on . . . anything that belongs to your neighbor'" (Deut. 5:21 NIV).

David had broken one of God's laws. He had coveted what someone else had.

Truth 2: Voicing his craving was not wise.

David usually watched his words fairly well. But in this case, what he said could have led to tragedy.

When he wished aloud for the water, who did he think would bring it? The Philistines? No, he didn't really expect to get any water at all. He certainly didn't want his men to risk their lives for it.

Knowing his desire could not be fulfilled immediately, David should have put it on hold for a time. But instead of saying no to that desire, he nurtured it until something that should never have been said popped out of his mouth.

As a result, David learned from experience the truth his son Solomon would later pen: "There is more hope for a stupid fool than for someone who speaks without thinking" (Prov. 29:20 TEV).

Truth 3: The risk was not worth the gain.

What had David gained? One drink of water. What might he have lost? Three of his best men. David didn't have to do much weighing to realize the scales didn't balance at all. Not all the water in all the wells in Israel would have been worth the loss of one of those lives.

Truth 4: Faithful friends cannot be too highly valued.

Focusing on something out of reach that he thought valuable, David failed to see the far more precious treasure under his nose. He failed, that is, until after the breakthrough. Then, the three stood before him, their outstretched hands holding the water for which he'd cried, their eyes shining. And he saw it: these men had courage and strength to defeat whole armies single-handedly, and they loved him so much they were willing to sacrifice their very lives to bring him pleasure.

So why didn't David show his appreciation by drinking from the cup the men brought? Drinking would show appreciation for the *water*. In light of the new lessons he'd learned, David wanted to show his appreciation for the *men*.

Furthermore, by refusing to drink, David refused to feed his craving. He may have known that indulging a wrong desire does not satisfy it, but rather causes it to grow.

Suppose David had chosen to drink that water. Probably, he would have felt guilty for a while for endangering his men by his rash remark. But gradually, he'd have begun to get thirsty for Bethlehem water again. Then, he would battle the temptation to *mention* his thirst again. He might have rationalized, "My men want to please me. They got the water the first time without getting hurt. Surely they can do it once more."

One day, David would have mentioned his renewed craving and in so doing multiplied his guilt and perhaps reaped disaster. Knowing how much the first gift of water had pleased him, how many of his men might have set out to get him a second helping? How many might have been killed?

But David didn't drink the water. He crushed his craving by denying it. In pouring the water out before the Lord, he showed his unspeakable appreciation for the men who had brought it and he broke the cycle. He would not again risk people to gain things.

The Right Teacher

Each breakthrough will yield different lessons. Some, like David's, may teach you the value of people or the hazards of sin. Others may confront you with a new understanding of Who God is. A breakthrough may reveal an attitude you need to change or a truth you need to embrace. It may open up a relationship you need to cultivate or start you on a path you need to take.

To learn the right lessons from any breakthrough, you must have the right Teacher. That Teacher is God the Spirit, Who indwells every believer. If you are a Christian, Jesus has promised that the Holy Spirit "will teach you all things" (John 14:26b NASB). But like any student, you choose whether to pay attention to the teacher or not. In fact, you can choose to learn from God's Spirit right now.

Recall a breakthrough you've experienced. Take time to ask, "Lord, what did You want me to learn from that?" After you've asked, and paused to allow God time to speak, take note of the thoughts that come to mind.

Remember, you're sitting under the Master Teacher. In His classroom, learning involves at least two aspects:

(1) Gaining or reinforcing understanding or insight. You *know* something new or see something you already knew in a fresh light.

(2) Applying what you now know. You *do* something. You respond. You change.

Once you realize one or more lessons that God intended you to learn from a breakthrough, seek to find how well you've learned them. Ask God to help you see yourself clearly. Then decide, Do I have the new perspectives God intended? How has my behavior changed to line up with those perspectives? Were the changes short-term or are they continuing?

If you've encountered breakthrough but your outlook and actions haven't changed at all, or changed for the worse, or changed for a while and then reverted to their old patterns, you almost surely didn't learn all God's Spirit wanted to teach you.

New Outlook, New Actions

From early childhood, Ron felt something was missing from his life. By age 24, he'd tried everything he thought might fill the void, including drugs, alcohol, gangs, marriage, and children. He spent 11 years in the drug culture, several of those as a heroin addict. He says, "I shot people; I stabbed people; I ran drugs to prison."

At 17, Ron married a Christian girl named Carol. The couple had a daughter, then a son. By the time his son was 2 years old, Ron needed a fix six times a day just to stay well, and even more often to get high.

One day, he and his friend Max visited a massage parlor that fronted for a dope ring. Leaving the parlor, Max saw another friend, Leroy, in a nearby parking lot. When Ron noticed the Jesus stickers on Leroy's truck he told Max, "I don't want to see him. I just want to get a fix." But Max insisted on walking over to Leroy's truck.

Leroy had led a life as rough or rougher than Ron's, but Leroy had accepted Jesus as his Lord and Saviour. Afterward, he turned himself in for 27 felonies. His life had changed so miraculously that local newspapers printed articles about him.

Leroy was in that parking lot that day on his way to have some tracts printed. He began witnessing to Max, "God loves you, Max, just like you are. If you'll just open up your heart and let Christ come in, He'll change you."

Though Leroy wasn't speaking to Ron, God was. Ron says, "I decided then to look to see if there was a God. I told my wife we were going to church."

The couple started attending church, and though Ron continued to feel God's tug, he resisted. Furthermore, Satan began distorting the truths Ron was hearing. Ron began to believe he could kill anybody he wanted and it wouldn't be wrong.

Carol could see that God was dealing with her husband. About a month after the two started going to church, she encouraged him to call the pastor and set up a meeting. Ron did. He and Carol walked into Pastor Bill's office on a Monday evening.

Ron says, "You need to know what I looked like. I had tattoos on my arms. I didn't know how to talk without cussing. I had hair down my back and a full beard. I had on my cleanest pair of dirty levis and a big knife on my hip. I'd cuss and then apologize for cussing. The pastor said, 'You don't have to apologize for being yourself. God loves you just the way you are.'"

Suddenly, Ron realized Leroy had said the same thing: "God loves you just the way you are." It seemed too that the pastor had the same spirit as Leroy. Ron and Carol talked and prayed with Pastor Bill for four hours that evening.

During the conversation, the pastor asked, "When will you next need a fix?"

"Five in the morning," Ron answered.

"I'm going to get up and pray for you at 5:00 A.M. while you're fixing," Bill said.

And he did. In fact, the pastor got up and prayed for Ron at 5:00 A.M. every day for the next week.

At the end of that week, Ron and his family went to visit a cousin. Ron told his cousin, "I'm planning to kill some people." Ron had made a list and he'd convinced himself that what he was planning was all right.

Overhearing Ron's plans, Carol decided to take the children and leave him as soon as they got home and he passed out. "Instead," says Ron, "when we got home, she fell asleep."

That night, for the first time in his life, Ron felt a sense of sin and a conviction of guilt that overwhelmed him. He took his Bible and drove to a field near his house. Parking under a eucalyptus tree, he turned on the dome light and began reading the Bible. He describes himself at that point as "a raving maniac." Upset, confused, and hopeless, he planned to take an overdose of drugs the next day.

His life had gone so far down the wrong track, he felt he could not change. He says, "There in that car, I heard a voice telling me, 'Put your faith in Me, and not in a needle, and I'll do it for you.'"

That night, Ron invited Jesus to be his Lord. He told the Lord he wanted only one thing: to kick the heroin habit. He says, "I immediately felt peace. From that night, my life has not been the same."

Ron recalls sitting on the edge of the bed at 9:00 the next morning, waking Carol and telling her, "It's going to be OK." Instead of feeling relieved, Carol became even more frightened. A psychiatrist had told her, "Ron is capable of killing you. Be aware that one warning signal is calm before the storm." Fearing Ron's new calm might be both deceptive and deadly, Carol watched him closely for weeks.

But Ron remained the new person he'd changed into overnight. He never had another fix. He says, "I never had withdrawal pains. I kept waiting, knowing they'd come. But they didn't." He had only one problem in kicking the heroin habit: for a month, he couldn't sleep. During that month, he read through the New Testament three times.

At the time of his conversion, Ron was making about $72,000 a year as a carpenter. Three years later, he decided to follow God's leading into full-time ministry. Stepping out in faith, he went back to school. While there, he made only $6,000 a year.

Ron got a bachelor's and master's degree in social work. Today, he is a licensed clinical social worker with an office in Fresno, California. He counsels adolescents and adults who need help in a variety of areas including their personal lives, their marriages, and drug rehabilitation. Since he receives his pay from a mission board, Ron offers his services free. He serves as chaplain for a county probation department and an areawide Bureau of Narcotics Enforcement, and leads retreats focusing on such subjects as time management and marriage enrichment.

Coming face-to-face with Jesus Christ, Ron experienced breakthrough. Instead of taking a step or two in the right direction, then reverting to the old way again, Ron turned 180 degrees; and he's still going in the right direction.

His life today is built on two truths he learned in the days after his salvation experience:

(1) Jesus alone can fill the void. The emptiness Ron had felt left the night he invited Jesus into his heart and never returned. Ron says, "I finally realized the void was a 'God spot.' Now, God Himself lives there."

Ron can't keep quiet about it. He says, "I share Christ with people wherever I go because, for me, on January 27, 1973, I fell hopelessly, helplessly, irreversibly in love with Jesus."

(2) God's Word can answer life's questions. The month Ron read the New Testament three times he found out what God expected from him, as well as what he could expect from God. Ron continues to make Bible reading a daily habit. "Being in the Word," he says, "is the thing that sees me through life's traumas."

Lesson of the Open Door

Will the Soviet peoples learn from the breakthrough that shocked the world? Some will never have any idea what God was trying to teach them. They won't see a Bible, read a tract, or meet a believer who can give them insight. Others will have access to the truth and reject it.

But some will learn. How many? That may well depend on how many hear. Will the people to whom I spoke on Red Square learn from breakthrough? Some won't; but, at least briefly, they all heard one lesson God used earthshaking events to try to teach.

I stepped up on a box and told them that "the God we serve is Creator of heaven and earth. He is the one true God. He is almighty. The Bible reveals Him.

"A year ago, He called me to spend whatever it cost to travel from the United States to your country. He did not speak out loud to me. As I read the Bible, He spoke to me. The Bible says, 'Behold, I have put before you an open door which no one can shut.'

"This year, on August 19, it seemed that door had swung firmly shut. Hard-line Communist leaders had toppled your government. Tanks rolled through Moscow's streets.

"But God had promised. He is true. He is almighty. And on August 21, He opened the door again.

"God has opened the way for us to be here. But much more importantly, He has opened the way for all people to have what we otherwise could not have: God Himself living in us.

"When the one true God comes to live inside a person, the person knows true freedom. That person knows true abundance. That person knows new life that never ends.

"Yet, how can this happen? How can God live within people? God is holy. He is utterly pure. He cannot enter a place made impure by even *one* wrong thought or word or deed, and every one of us says and thinks and does *many* wrong things.

"Two thousand years ago, God made a way where there was none. He sent His Son Jesus to earth. The Bible says, 'In Jesus, all the fullness of God dwells in bodily form.' Jesus lived a perfectly pure life. Then, he died on a cross in our behalf.

"Three days after dying, Jesus rose again. He had opened the door that could not be opened—the door from death to life.

"In dying, He took every speck of our ugliness on Himself. Now, in exchange, He offers us His life and purity.

"Jesus Christ is the way. *He is the open door.* Because of Him, God can now live within you and me.

"But God will not force Himself on anyone. Though He can shatter any door, there is one door He will not open. That is the door to your heart. The Bible says, 'Behold, I stand at the door and knock; if anyone hears My voice and opens the door, I will come in to Him, and will dine with Him, and he with Me.'

"Jesus has opened the way for the Soviet peoples to hear the truth about Him. If you have not opened your heart's door to Jesus Christ, won't you do so today?"

Lesson Learned?

I stepped down from the box and Andrea sang "Jesus Loves Me." People cried. Lisa, the one missions team member who spoke fluent Russian, gave her testimony. The crowd listened intently.

Stepping back onto the box, Andrea briefly explained how to receive new life in Christ. She also announced that we had New Testaments for everyone after the service.

Then, scanning the faces of the people circled around us, she asked anyone who would make a decision to receive Jesus today to step forward. First one person moved; then another; and then the whole crowd pressed forward, engulfing those of us who stood ready to hand out the Bibles we held.

How many of those people were actually committing their lives to Christ? How many of them were crowding forward to get a Bible or were simply moved forward by the crowd? We don't know, but God does. He sees the heart response. He knows exactly who has learned from breakthrough.

10

LORD OF BREAKTHROUGH

*"One who breaks open the way will go up before
them; they will break through the gate and go out.
Their king will pass through before them,
the Lord at their head"
(Mic. 2:13 NIV).*

It was Sunday in Yalta. On Monday, we would fly back to Moscow; the day after, we would fly home to the US. My roommate Donna had gone to bed Saturday night grief-stricken over her brother Elijah's death and guilt-ridden because she had made the trip to the Soviet Union at a time her family needed her so badly.

She woke up a different person. In answer to our Saturday night prayer session, God had worked. Certainly, Donna still felt grief, but the guilt had vanished. She was bubbly again, full of smiles, and eager to be about the work she'd come to do.

She began the day talking about Alla, the tour guide who had traveled with our group to Yalta. Alla, a Russian Jew, had never before encountered a Christian tour group. She seemed touched by what she'd seen and heard all week.

Alla translated for us during our Enterprisers evangelistic service on Red Square; and she cried. The times we handed out Bibles, she jumped off the bus with the rest of us, grabbed her own armload of New Testaments and moved out among the people, offering them to whomever she saw.

One or two members of our group spoke with Alla during the

week about what it meant to receive Jesus. She listened and seemed interested, but made no commitment. "I believe God wants me to talk to Alla," Donna told me that Sunday morning. "He's really put her on my heart."

Later that same day, Alla sought out Donna and told her, "I saw you crying yesterday. I've never prayed before, but I prayed for you last night."

Our bus pulled out of Yalta Monday morning. After the two-hour drive to Simferopol, we boarded the Aeroflot jet that would take us back to Moscow. On board, Donna sat next to Alla and talked to her about becoming a Christian. Alla told Donna, "I'm ready in my heart, but not in my head." That night, back at the Cosmos Hotel in Moscow, Donna got out the English Bible and the letter her brother Elijah had entrusted to her. She gave them to Alla.

The next morning, we were to have our luggage standing ready at the door of our hotel room by 6:00. The porter knocked on our door at 6:00 sharp. Donna and I both jumped straight out of bed. She thought I had set the alarm; I thought she had.

Peeking out the door, I told the porter (in Russian), "Five minutes." He had no other luggage on his cart. We assumed he would move on down the hall collecting the bags and then return to our room before leaving the floor.

Hurrying into our clothes and throwing everything into our large suitcases except what we wanted to carry on the plane, we had the bags ready to go before the five minutes were up. I hoisted my suitcase, threw open the door . . . and almost ran into the porter and his cart. He was still standing exactly where he stood when I opened the door the first time. We handed him the two suitcases, tipped him, and fell back into the room to try to get ourselves together before breakfast.

Three minutes later, Donna realized she had left her airplane tickets in her suitcase. She stepped out into the hall, but the porter had vanished. "I'm going to try to catch him downstairs," she told me.

To get where the luggage would eventually end up, Donna had to take the elevator from our eighth-floor room to the basement level. All the bags would be gathered there and loaded onto our buses for the trip to the airport.

Once in the basement, Donna retrieved her tickets. Then she saw Alla walking toward her with a big smile on her face. When she reached Donna, Alla said, "Because of the Bible and the letter, I have become a Christian."

Donna had not read her brother's letter. The envelope was addressed "To whoever receives this Bible." She felt it was a private message. Alla told her, "The letter was so clear. It was so simple. It answered all my questions."

Seeing God's Picture in Breakthrough

How well do you know the Lord of breakthrough? If you belong to Him, you've glimpsed Him; but like all believers, you always need to know Him better. Do you *long* to know Him better?

If you will look, you can see something of His acts and His ways by examining a few pictures of breakthrough He has scattered through His Word. But remember, those who see Him are accountable to respond to Him. And indeed, you *will* respond to Him in one way or another.

A Split Rock: God's Provision

While they were camped in the desert, en route to the Promised Land from Egypt, the Israelites had no water. What did they do? They quarreled with Moses; they grumbled against Moses. Apparently, the thought that "we need to pray about this" never crossed their minds.

But the thought did cross Moses' mind. He cried out to God, and God told him what to do: "Take in your hand the staff with which you struck the Nile, and go. I will stand there before you by the rock at Horeb. Strike the rock, and water will come out of it for the people to drink" (Ex. 17:5b-6 NIV).

Moses did what God said; he struck the rock. Hundreds of years later, Isaiah recalled what God did next: "He split the rock, and the water gushed forth" (Isa. 48:21b NASB).

The Lord performed a miracle to show a quarreling, grumbling people that He is Provider. How did they respond? They thanked Him by grumbling and rebelling some more. When He supplied water, they started complaining about their lack of food. The lesson of the split rock passed right over their heads.

Lori's Provider

When Lori was a high school senior, she served on a cheerleading squad that was scheduled to take part in a national competition.

Wednesday before the competition was to be held on Saturday, the girl who was to be at the top of the pyramid got sick. A girl from another squad stepped in to replace her. The cheerleaders told her,

"Fall back from the top of the pyramid, and we'll catch you. Don't push off. Just fall back."

Once atop the pyramid, the girl became nervous. She pushed off, and went rocketing toward the floor, head first. Lori and another cheerleader ran to catch her. The hurtling girl hit Lori in the face, breaking her nose and cheekbone, crushing the disks in both jaws. Lori hit the floor, fractured her skull, and suffered a concussion.

Surgery to put "cadaver disks" in her jaws left the right side of her face paralyzed. Among other things, she could not blink her right eye. To keep the eye from drying out, she had to blink her eye by hand, and to tape her eyelid shut when she went out in the wind.

In follow-up surgery, doctors took a nerve from Lori's leg, removed the nerve from her face, and ran the nerve from the "good" side to her chin, lip, and eye on the paralyzed side. They waited six months to see if the nerve would give life to the right side of her face; it did. A third surgery was required when Lori's body began to reject the cadaver disks in her jaws.

Since the first day of the accident, she has not been able to breathe out of the left side of her nose. Also, in spite of prayer and every treatment possible, she has suffered severe, unrelieved headaches. On a scale of one to ten, where one is minor discomfort and ten is migraine-type pain that wakes a person up at night and causes sick stomachs, Lori's head has hurt not less than an eight since the day of the accident.

For almost a year, Lori was a recluse. She stayed in her room and spent much time reading her Bible. Then one day, the 19-year-old walked out of her bedroom and into the room where her dad was sitting. She said, "Dad, I believe that with God there's an answer for every problem. But I believe the answer is sometimes learning how to live with the problem."

At age 23, Lori graduated from college with a bachelor's degree in social work. She is now working to get her master's and doctorate degrees. She plans to be an industrial psychologist with a private practice on the side.

God has provided for Lori, not by giving complete healing, but with a breakthrough of wisdom and grace to live a full life in spite of her pain. Unlike the Israelites of old, Lori has responded not only by accepting what God offered but also by trusting her Lord to continue to provide.

Split Ranks in Battle: God's Name

It's a war story with a twist. The Israelite nation was divided. Godly King Jehoshaphat ruled the Southern Kingdom, Judah. Jehoram, son of the notorious king Ahab, ruled the Northern Kingdom, Israel. Almost as wicked as his father, Jehoram led Israel to do everything but worship the true God.

Mesha, king of Moab, rebelled against Israel. When he quit supplying King Jehoram the lambs and wool he had promised, Jehoram decided to attack Moab. He enlisted Jehoshaphat, as well as the king of neighboring Edom, to go into battle with him.

On the way to attack Moab, the three armies ran out of water. At Jehoshaphat's request, the three kings consulted the prophet Elisha. Because Jehoshaphat was involved, Elisha approached the Lord and then announced God's plan: "'Make this valley full of ditches. For this is what the Lord says: You will see neither wind nor rain, yet this valley will be filled with water. . . . This is an easy thing in the eyes of the Lord; he will also hand Moab over to you'" (2 Kings 3:16b-18 NIV).

The soldiers dug the ditches, and the Lord filled them with water. The next morning, when the Moabites saw the sun shining red on water that had not been there the night before, they jumped to a wrong conclusion. Thinking the three armies had slaughtered each other, the Moabites set out not for battle, but for a mop-up operation. They were routed before the three combined (and refreshed) armies.

Israel and her allies then invaded Moab, devastating it. But they could not take Kir Hareseth, Moab's major city and King Mesha's refuge. In a last desperate attempt to oust the invaders, Mesha and 700 swordsmen came out of the city and tried to "break through to the king of Edom" (2 Kings 3:26c NIV), presumably the weakest of the three kings. But Mesha's attack failed. He could not break through. He and his men were forced back behind the city walls.

Analyzing the battle, Mesha decided his army had suffered defeat because his gods were angry with him. To appease gods who didn't exist, he offered his firstborn son, the heir to his throne, as a burnt offering on the city wall. Reporting the tragedy, the Bible makes an odd statement: "The fury against Israel was great; they withdrew and returned to their own land" (2 Kings 3:27b NIV).

The Moabite king committed the atrocity. Yet, fury broke out against Israel. Why? To gain insight here, let's answer three questions:

(1) What was the turning point in the three kings' assault? Surely, the miracle of the water-filled ditches.

(2) Who sent the water and gave the victory? The Lord God, of course.

(3) And now, the key question: What should have happened in Moab as a result? The Scriptures indicate that whenever the Lord acted mightily in behalf of Israel, He intended for pagan nations to know He alone was God. The miracle of the water should have made the Lord's name known to His enemies.

But when King Mesha tried to figure out what went wrong in the battle, he apparently never considered that Israel's God might be involved and that He might be greater than the idols Mesha worshiped. Why? Perhaps because at that time the Israelites gave no evidence that God was their God. They had separated themselves from temple worship. They were making their own rules and changing those rules whenever they wanted. They were a people in rebellion.

Looking at Israel, Mesha would have seen no reason for a holy God to act on their behalf. And indeed, Elisha made clear that God would not have acted had it not been for godly King Jehoshaphat of Judah.

Because of Israel's evil reputation, the God Who gave the victory did not receive the glory. The One Who prevented a last-minute enemy breakthrough didn't get the credit. Because of the decadence of God's people, a pagan father sacrificed his son to invented idols rather than bowing before the one true God. No wonder Israel returned home not defeated, but shamed.

Whenever the Lord sends or withholds breakthrough on behalf of His people, His name is at stake. If, because of our ungodly lives, others cannot recognize His working, tragedy and shame will result.

Flood: God's Wrath

"The Lord has broken through my enemies before me like the breakthrough of waters," cried David after a major victory over the Philistines. His phrase, "breakthrough of waters," describes a flood.

Water usually symbolizes life. We drink water, bathe in it, boil it for sterilizing, and pour it over our plants. Yet, when contained waters break through their container, what once gave and sustained life destroys it. What once lapped at the land overtakes it with devastating, relentless, sweeping power . . . power that cannot be withstood.

Of course, floods are natural disasters that occur in a fallen world. They do not necessarily indicate God's judgment against a certain place or people. Yet flood waters picture a spiritual truth: the same

Lord Who gives life, cleansing, and refreshing is God of power and wrath. Once unleashed, His wrath can wreak devastating destruction. It cannot be withstood.

Physical floods may seem to hit without rhyme or reason. Conversely, God does not unleash the flood of His anger arbitrarily or without forethought. Even in wrath, He is righteous.

When God vented His power in David's behalf, God was not taking David's side; rather David had placed himself on God's side. David's experience illustrates a truth Nahum declared: "The Lord takes vengeance on *His adversaries*, and He reserves wrath for *His enemies*" (Nah. 1:2*b* NASB, italics mine).

The Hebrew word for *enemies* in that verse means "to be hostile to." It describes persons who have set themselves against someone else. God doesn't just decide that some people are His enemies, then treat them accordingly. Rather He counts as His adversaries all whose actions and attitudes show hostility toward Him. He counts as friends all who yield themselves to Him.

Even God's people can act with hostility toward Him, and thus set themselves against Him. Of the Israelites Isaiah said, "Yet they rebelled and grieved his Holy Spirit. So he turned and became their enemy and he himself fought against them" (Isa. 63:10 NIV).

To believers James wrote, "You adulteresses, do you not know that friendship with the world is hostility toward God? Therefore whoever wishes to be a friend of the world makes himself an enemy of God" (James 4:4 NASB).

No matter how close you stay to God, He may allow you to experience natural disasters or other kinds of trauma or crisis. No person who lives in this fallen world can escape such difficulties. But if you are a Christian, you do not ever have to experience God's wrath. Live in a state of yieldedness to the Lord Jesus Christ. Then, when God's anger does break through, His devastation will be turned not against you, but in your behalf.

Hatching Eggs: God's Life

Try to find Edom on a modern map. You can look all day, but you won't locate the tiny Middle East kingdom. Edom isn't there anymore.

In Old Testament times, the Edomites made themselves God's enemies. God promised to unleash His wrath against them. In fact, the prophet Isaiah foretold what our maps confirm: Edom's devastation would be complete; its destruction, total. Isaiah declared that the country would lie desolate "from generation to generation" (Isa. 34:10b NIV). The area would resemble the world prior to God's creation; it would be formless and void.

No person would live there, or even pass through. Only desert creatures such as jackals, hyenas, wild goats, and falcons would inhabit the place. Isaiah said, "The owl will nest there and lay eggs, she will hatch them, and care for her young under the shadow of her wings" (Isa. 34:15a NIV).

Wait a minute. Isaiah said what? Writing of death, the prophet suddenly painted a gentle scene of tender relationship and quiet breakthrough to life. The mother and her babies are not human. In fact, they're not even "clean" animals in Jewish thinking; but they are living creatures.

God is the God of life. When the earth was "formless and void," the Lord couldn't leave it that way. He went to work and didn't quit until the dark, desolate place was teeming with life.

When He unleashes His wrath, His fury may reduce everything in its path to its precreation state; but after the explosive breakthrough of His anger will always come the quiet breakthrough of His life. Even the utter devastation of the final judgment will be prelude to a new heaven and a new earth, peopled with all those to whom God has given His life.

Remember: God is life. When you see His wrath loosed, stay alert for the hatching to follow.

Childbirth: God's Grace

Perez had three strikes against him. He was the second-born of twins; his mother, Tamar, was not married when he was conceived; he was a child of incest.

Judah, Perez's father, had three legitimate sons. The two older sons were wicked. The eldest married a young woman named Tamar. Before long, he died. Judah gave Tamar to the second son. Before long, he died.

Judah's third son was much younger than the other two. Judah told Tamar to live as a widow in his house until Shelah, the third son, grew up. According to Jewish custom, Tamar would then become Shelah's bride.

Judah had no intention of giving Tamar to his only living son. He feared the death pattern might repeat itself. When Tamar saw that Judah planned to leave her a childless widow, she disguised herself as a prostitute, met Judah along the way on a trip he was taking, and lay with him. As a result, she conceived.

Later, learning his daughter-in-law was pregnant, Judah ordered that she be killed. Tamar produced the personal items Judah had given her when he lay with her. At that point, Judah admitted his own wrongdoing in the matter and allowed Tamar to live.

Soon she gave birth to twin boys. "While she was in labor, one of them put out an arm; the midwife caught it, tied a red thread around it, and said, 'This one was born first.' But he pulled his arm back, and his brother was born first. Then the midwife said, 'So this is how you break your way out!'" (Gen. 38:28-29 TEV).

The baby who pushed his way out was named Perez, meaning "breakthrough." According to the Jewish system of reckoning such things, Perez had no claim to the family blessing or the birthright. Those were passed down to legitimate, firstborn sons.

Yet, three biblical genealogies show that God gave Perez a family birthright and blessing surpassing any other. Ruth 4 names Perez as a forefather of King David, and the Gospels of Matthew and Luke list Perez in the direct lineage of Jesus Christ.

When Perez's tiny fist appeared out of the order of his birth, it symbolized a greater breakthrough the Lord was going to do in his life, a breakthrough of grace. God was going to make Judah's son of sin a forefather of the Redeemer.

Today, the God of grace is still accomplishing breakthrough on behalf of people who do not deserve it. He delights in taking bad backgrounds, undesirable situations, and confessed sins, and turning them to good in the lives of those who love Him.

Rain Clouds: God's Presence

Ominous clouds gather overhead. You just know that any minute "the bottom will drop out." The rain will burst through its filmy holders and spill out on the earth. If the clouds pass without dumping their contents, you're amazed.

Ominous situations gather. You just know that any minute break-through will occur. Someone or something will burst under the pressure, and a torrent will result. Even though the outpouring may be harsh, you'll welcome it, for the tension is so great. If the occasion passes without incident, you're amazed.

Amazement in such situations is natural, but don't let it lead to disillusionment. Whether you're facing rain clouds or facing stormy situations, never decide that absence of breakthrough signals the absence of God. God is present when the clouds gather, and when they stay, and stay, and stay. In fact, clouds often symbolized God's presence in the Old Testament.

Through the pillar of cloud, God directed the Israelites in their wilderness wanderings. God descended in a cloud on the tabernacle and, later, the Temple. Once when David cried for help, God came to his rescue in a dark cloud.

The God Who wraps Himself in clouds is a hidden God. No one can see His form. No one can fully know Him. Yet He is present. He is there when breakthrough seems imminent, but does not come.

He is not only present, but also in control. Never decide that the absence of breakthrough means the Lord just can't bring it about. Often, more power is needed to hold back breakthrough than to loose it; and the same God Who unleashes has the strength to withhold.

As one of Job's friends testified, "It is God who fills the clouds with water and keeps them from bursting with the weight" (Job 26:8 TEV).

Dawn: God's Promise
Somewhere in the world right now it's midnight. Most places, though, it's not. In those other places, it's morning, high noon, or dusk, or it's one of the dark hours moving toward or away from midnight. Still, it's midnight everywhere, sometime. If it's not the stroke of 12:00 where you are, wait an hour, or 2, or 10, or 20. Midnight will come.

But it will also pass. It never hangs around anywhere long. Oh, the darkness lingers and may even seem to grow deeper. Look outside and you'll swear midnight is here to stay; but look at the clock and you'll know. Time has rounded the corner; it's heading relentlessly toward . . . dawn.

Daybreak comes in the physical realm just as surely as midnight. The promise of its coming has carried many a person through a long night. In the spiritual realm, God gives promises of dawn that are just as sure.

The Apostle Peter urged his readers to pay attention to prophecy "because it is like a lamp shining in a dark place until the Day dawns" (2 Pet. 1:19b TEV). Peter knew the morning was coming.

To the wayward Israelites Isaiah said, "Then your light will break out like the dawn. . . . Then your light will rise in darkness" (Isa. 58:8a,10b NASB). Speaking for God, He promised the breakthrough of sunrise. But Isaiah made another point: spiritually speaking, dawn comes only to those who put themselves in the path of its approach.

The same principle holds true physically. Dawn will come to you anywhere, if you don't run from it. But if you start in a place of darkness and move west with the night, you will never know sunrise.

The Israelites had known a long night, but much of it was their own fault. By continually chasing their own desires, they kept following the darkness. Only when they stood still and began giving themselves to meet others' needs would they see the dawn.

My friend Andrea put herself in the path of daybreak at one point during our Soviet Union trip. She relates her story:

"We were on our way from Moscow to Bishkek. At the airport, we had one more passport and luggage check to go through. Checking the passports was a military woman seated at a desk in the drab room through which we were passing. One volunteer described her as the "iron maiden." She was large and stern, dressed in a military uniform. She looked up at me with the same sober eyes and stern expression I had observed all over Moscow. As I looked into her face, I thought this was a woman who had no interest in God. I smiled at her, but she didn't respond in turn. So I passed on by her and started into the next waiting room.

"But God's Spirit stopped me and urged me to go back to her. I reached into my bag, pulled out a Bible, held it out to her, and said, 'Biblia.' She shook her head and told me in Russian that she did not know English. I said, 'Nyet, nyet, pah Rushkie' ('No, no, it's Russian').

"She took off her glasses and laid them on the desk. She picked up the Bible and began to read. She read for nearly a minute while I stood and watched. She would read for a few seconds, then turn the page and read some more. I thought she was about to rail at me for giving her such a book.

"Then she looked up at me. Tears were streaming down her face. She stood up, raised her arms high into the air, and began praising God in Russian. Her eyes were filled with joy and gratitude. Her hard face was transformed by a smile that stretched from cheek to cheek. Without any concern for what others may think, she was praising God and telling the other military in the room about her Bible. She reached out to me, hugging me and expressing her gratitude over and over. When I looked back at her as I left the room, she was going from soldier to soldier, reading from the Bible, laughing, crying, and praising God."

God promises dawn—and He sends it. But, those who experience God's daybreaks are those who follow the prompting of God's Spirit. They're those who stand in the darkness and wait for the light.

Honoring the Sovereign Lord

When I began preparing to write this book, I intended to have the manuscript completed by the end of summer 1991. I prayed, studied, and started gathering information and experiences. God let me make progress, but not nearly as much progress as I'd hoped.

I left for the Soviet Union on September 2, 1991 with much information gathered, but only one chapter written.

Until that trip, I had chafed because I was writing about breakthrough, and I couldn't seem to have one. Other obligations kept pushing work on the manuscript aside.

I returned from the Soviet Union recognizing why God had withheld breakthrough in my book writing. He needed to teach me some things firsthand before I could put them on paper. During that trip, I experienced in awesome ways each of the aspects of breakthrough I had planned to include in the book. More than that, I learned that to seek breakthrough is not nearly as important as to seek and to know the Lord of breakthrough.

If you're needy and He splits a rock, revere Him as God the Provider. If you're defeated and He gives victory, shout aloud the honor of His name. To avoid the taste of His wrath, make sure you are His ally. Alienate yourself from whomever and whatever sets itself against Him.

To experience His nurturing life, cling to Him, even in the desert places. As a mother delights in her newborn, delight in His grace. Regardless of whether or not life's clouds produce rain, depend on His presence. As you greet each new day, claim His promises.

Remember, whatever the circumstances, our God is Lord of *breakthrough*. He can burst through barriers, even "impossible" barriers, to accomplish His purposes in individual lives and in His world.

Our God is *Lord* of breakthrough. He works how He will, when He will. He chooses to allow His people to limit and to shape His workings. But always, ultimately, He rules.

Who, after all, could use a deceased man of faith named Elijah, an English Bible, a letter, and an obedient sister to win a Russian Jew named Alla to Christ? The *Lord of Breakthrough!*

NOTES

Introduction
[1]George J. Church, "Anatomy of a Coup," *Time*, September 2, 1991, 36.

Chapter 1. WHERE THERE'S A WALL, THERE'S A WAY
[1]George J. Church, "Freedom!" *Time*, November 20, 1989, 26.
[2]Stephen Budiansky, "And the Wall Came Tumbling Down," *U.S. News & World Report*, November 20, 1989, 9.

Chapter 2. WHY SO FEW BREAKTHROUGHS?
[1]Charles Colson, *Against the Night* (Ann Arbor, MI: Servant Publications, 1989), 107-8.
[2]Ibid., 109.

Chapter 5. BREAKTHROUGH!
[1]Christopher Bobinski, "The Gathering Storms," *U.S. News & World Report*, October 28, 1991, 59.
[2]Art Toalston, "Soviet Events Trigger 'Green Alert' at FMB," *The Baptist Record*, September 12, 1991, 1.
[3]Karen Benson, "Miracles in the Soviet Union," *Royal Service*, February 1992, 25.

Chapter 6. WHEN BREAKTHROUGH HURTS
[1]Catherine B. Allen, *The New Lottie Moon Story* (Nashville: Broadman Press, 1980), 48.

Chapter 8. CLOSING THE BREACHES
[1]Watchman Nee, *The Release of the Spirit* (Indianapolis: Sure Foundation Publishers, 1965), 19.
[2]Ibid., 45.
[3]Ibid., 63.
[4]Ibid., 61.
[5]Ibid., 12-13.